영어 피트니스
50일의 기적 3

— 원서 읽기 편 —

BEYOND
A·L·L

영어 피트니스 50일의 기적 3

초판 1쇄 발행 2015년 12월 7일
초판 2쇄 발행 2015년 12월 24일

지은이 정회일
펴낸이 김선식

경영총괄 김은영
마케팅총괄 최창규
책임편집 이여홍 **책임마케터** 박현미
콘텐츠개발3팀장 김서윤 **콘텐츠개발3팀** 이여홍, 김규림, 최수아
마케팅본부 이주화, 정명찬, 이상혁, 최혜령, 박현미, 김선욱, 이소연
경영관리팀 송현주, 윤이경, 권송이, 임해랑
외부스태프 교정교열 김소현 **디자인** 디자인86

펴낸곳 다산북스 **출판등록** 2005년 12월 23일 제313-2005-00277호
주소 경기도 파주시 회동길 37-14 3, 4층
전화 02-702-1724(기획편집) 02-6217-1726(마케팅) 02-704-1724(경영관리)
팩스 02-703-2219 **이메일** dasanbooks@dasanbooks.com
홈페이지 www.dasanbooks.com **블로그** blog.naver.com/dasan_books
종이 한솔 **출력·제본** 갑우문화사 **후가공** 갑우문화사

ⓒ 2015, 정회일

ISBN 979-11-306-0667-5(14740)
SET 979-11-306-0664-4(14740)

- 책값은 뒤표지에 있습니다.
- 파본은 구입하신 서점에서 교환해드립니다.
- 이 책은 저작권법에 의하여 보호를 받는 저작물이므로 무단 전재와 복제를 금합니다.
- 이 도서의 국립중앙도서관 출판시도서목록(CIP)은 서지정보유통지원시스템 홈페이지(http://seoji.nl.go.kr)와 국가자료공동목록시스템(http://www.nl.go.kr/kolisnet)에서 이용하실 수 있습니다.

다산북스(DASANBOOKS)는 독자 여러분의 책에 관한 아이디어와 원고 투고를 기쁜 마음으로 기다리고 있습니다. 책 출간을 원하는 아이디어가 있으신 분은 이메일 dasanbooks@dasanbooks.com 또는 다산북스 홈페이지 '투고원고'란으로 간단한 개요와 취지, 연락처 등을 보내주세요. 머뭇거리지 말고 문을 두드리세요.

머리말

'원서 읽기!' 혹은 '공공 장소에서 원서 읽기'는 많은 한국인들이 꿈꾸는 일 중 하나지 싶습니다. 저에게도 그랬고요. 남들 보는 데서 원어민과 영어로 대화하기, 영어로 통화하기도 멋지지만 원서를 폼 나게 읽고 있는 거도 참 멋지죠.

저도 그렇게 하고 싶어 수년간 원서를 '읽는 척'을 했는데, 참 이게 쉽지가 않았습니다. 초기엔 단어 문제인 줄 알았는데 단어를 많이 익히고 나서도 여전히 우리말 책 읽듯 읽히지가 않더라고요. 해서 또 많은 학습법을 연구했는데 이건 답도 안 나오더라고요. '그냥 많이 읽었다' 정도가 공통된 답이랄까… 영어를 알려주는 사람으로서 단지 그렇게만 말할 수는 없었습니다. 해서 또 엄청나게 깊이 생각하고 서적과 도서관에서 영어 책들을 노려보며 고민했습니다.

'영어로 된 책을 쉽게… 아니… 한 문장 읽을 때마다 앞뒤로 왔다 갔다 하며 이상한 번역하지 않고 정상적으로 순서대로 읽을 방법이 무엇일까?'에 대해 몇 달간을 고민하던 어느 날… 퍼뜩! 그림이 떠올랐습니다. 영문장의 구조를 쉽게 보여줄 방법이 떠오른 거죠. 해서 열심히 글로 작성하고, 테스트를 통해 책으로 만들게 되었네요. 개인적인 생각으론 이 책에서 사용한 영문장의 구조를 보여주는 방식이 아름답다 생각하는데요. 보는 분들은 어떨지 모르겠네요. 일단 도움은 분명히 될 겁니다!^^

이 책 원서 읽기 편에서는 그 많은 원서 중, 그 많은 한국인들이 도전해보는 바로 그!! The!! 저도 영어에 특별히 관심이 없었음에도 어렸을 적 어디서 굴러온 원서를 몇 번쯤 읽으려고 시도했던 그 책!! 《어린 왕자》로 연습하겠습니다. 이 책에 나오는 문장들은 원작에서 많이 손 보지 않았어요. 거의 동일한 레벨입니다. 도움 장치가 조금 있긴 하지만요. 이 책으로 일단 읽어보고 진짜 원서에도 도전해보세요. 그리고 꼭 1) 자기가 좋아하는 책을 '찾아' 2) 원서로 3) 반복해서 읽어보세요. 영어와 인생에 보탬이 될 거예요!

저는 이 책을 작업하면서 힘들기도 했지만 아주 즐거웠습니다. 여러분도 '생애 최초로' '제대로 읽어보는 어린 왕자 원서' 즐겁게 읽길 바랄게요. 즐거운 시간 보내세요! 여러분은, 우리는 행복하기 위해 태어났습니다. 행복하게 살아요 우리.^^

학습계획표

학습에 참고할 수 있도록 《원서 읽기》 4주 완성 학습계획표를 짰습니다. 이 학습계획표를 토대로 자신만의 학습 시간과 학습 수준에 맞는 계획을 세워 효과적인 학습 방법을 찾기 바랍니다.

	본문 학습 진도						복습
1주차	MON	TUE	WED	THU	FRI	SAT	SUN
DAY 1 ~ DAY 7	DAY 1 Step 1 원문 읽기 Step 2 구조 파악과 이해	DAY 2 Step 1 원문 읽기 Step 2 구조 파악과 이해	DAY 3 Step 1 원문 읽기 Step 2 구조 파악과 이해	DAY 4 Step 1 원문 읽기 Step 2 구조 파악과 이해	DAY 5 Step 1 원문 읽기 Step 2 구조 파악과 이해	DAY 6 Step 1 원문 읽기 Step 2 구조 파악과 이해	DAY 7 Step 3 1주차 지문을 한 번에 읽어봐요
2주차	MON	TUE	WED	THU	FRI	SAT	SUN
DAY 8 ~ DAY 14	DAY 8 Step 1 원문 읽기 Step 2 구조 파악과 이해	DAY 9 Step 1 원문 읽기 Step 2 구조 파악과 이해	DAY 10 Step 1 원문 읽기 Step 2 구조 파악과 이해	DAY 11 Step 1 원문 읽기 Step 2 구조 파악과 이해	DAY 12 Step 1 원문 읽기 Step 2 구조 파악과 이해	DAY 13 Step 1 원문 읽기 Step 2 구조 파악과 이해	DAY 14 Step 3 2주차 지문을 한 번에 읽어봐요
3주차	MON	TUE	WED	THU	FRI	SAT	SUN
DAY 15 ~ DAY 21	DAY 15 Step 1 원문 읽기 Step 2 구조 파악과 이해	DAY 16 Step 1 원문 읽기 Step 2 구조 파악과 이해	DAY 17 Step 1 원문 읽기 Step 2 구조 파악과 이해	DAY 18 Step 1 원문 읽기 Step 2 구조 파악과 이해	DAY 19 Step 1 원문 읽기 Step 2 구조 파악과 이해	DAY 20 Step 1 원문 읽기 Step 2 구조 파악과 이해	DAY 21 Step 3 2주차 지문을 한 번에 읽어봐요
4주차	MON	TUE	WED	THU	FRI	SAT	SUN
DAY 22 ~ DAY 28	DAY 22 Step 1 원문 읽기 Step 2 구조 파악과 이해	DAY 23 Step 1 원문 읽기 Step 2 구조 파악과 이해	DAY 24 Step 1 원문 읽기 Step 2 구조 파악과 이해	DAY 25 Step 1 원문 읽기 Step 2 구조 파악과 이해	DAY 26 Step 1 원문 읽기 Step 2 구조 파악과 이해	DAY 27 Step 1 원문 읽기 Step 2 구조 파악과 이해	DAY 28 Step 3 2주차 지문을 한 번에 읽어봐요

이 책의 구성

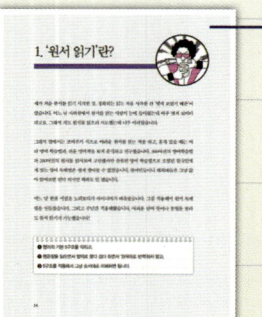

워밍업

본격적인 원서 읽기 훈련을 시작하기 전에 꼭 알고 넘어가야 할 내용을 미리 확인하세요.

Step 1 원문 읽기

오늘 연습할 내용을 친절한 설명과 함께 미리 한번 읽어보세요. 구조를 파악한 후 읽을 때와 비교할 수 있어요.

how to use this book

Step 2 구조 파악과 이해

영어의 5구조를 적용해서 문장의 구조를 파악해보세요.
(1) 문장의 기본 뼈대 인 주어+동사는 색깔로 표시해두었고, (2) 전치사+명사, (3) to+동사, (4) 동사가 변형된 분사, (5) 접속사는 각 구문에 번호로 표시해두었어요.

Step 3 한 번에 읽어보기

한 주 동안 연습한 내용을 한꺼번에 읽어보세요. 마치 진짜 원서를 읽는 것처럼요.

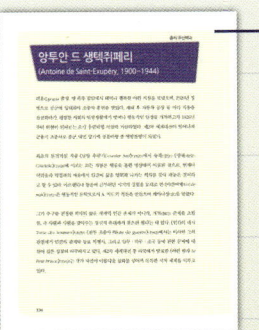

부록

작품에 대한 이해를 도와 학습에 참고할 수 있도록 《어린 왕자》에 대한 이야기를 실어두었습니다.

CONTENTS

머리말 _3

학습계획표 _5

이 책의 구성 _6

PART 1 워밍업

1. '원서 읽기'란? _14

2. 영어의 5구조 _16

3. 문법 공부는 이제 그만! _22

4. 직관적 리딩 _24

5. 원서 읽기 FAQ _26

PART 2 원서 읽기 훈련 코스
: 《어린 왕자》

Week 1

DAY 1 Once when I was six years old _35
STEP 1. 원문 읽기   STEP 2. 구조 파악과 이해

DAY 2 The grown-ups' response _41
STEP 1. 원문 읽기   STEP 2. 구조 파악과 이해

DAY 3 Then I would never talk to that person _47
STEP 1. 원문 읽기   STEP 2. 구조 파악과 이해

DAY 4 And I saw a most extraordinary small person _53
STEP 1. 원문 읽기   STEP 2. 구조 파악과 이해

DAY 5 When a mystery is too overpowering _59
STEP 1. 원문 읽기   STEP 2. 구조 파악과 이해

DAY 6 But it was rejected too _65
STEP 1. 원문 읽기   STEP 2. 구조 파악과 이해

DAY 7 STEP 3. 1주차 지문을 한 번에 읽어봐요 _71

Week 2

DAY 8 That is not an object _85
STEP 1. 원문 읽기   STEP 2. 구조 파악과 이해

DAY 9 That is so _91
STEP 1. 원문 읽기   STEP 2. 구조 파악과 이해

| DAY 10 | I have reason to believe | _97 |

STEP 1. 원문 읽기 STEP 2. 구조 파악과 이해

| DAY 11 | If you were to say to the grown-ups | _103 |

STEP 1. 원문 읽기 STEP 2. 구조 파악과 이해

| DAY 12 | Six years have already passed | _109 |

STEP 1. 원문 읽기 STEP 2. 구조 파악과 이해

| DAY 13 | As each day passed I would learn | _115 |

STEP 1. 원문 읽기 STEP 2. 구조 파악과 이해

| DAY 14 | STEP 3. 2주차 지문을 한 번에 읽어봐요 | _121 |

Week 3

| DAY 15 | There were good plants and bad plants | _135 |

STEP 1. 원문 읽기 STEP 2. 구조 파악과 이해

| DAY 16 | And one day he said to me | _141 |

STEP 1. 원문 읽기 STEP 2. 구조 파악과 이해

| DAY 17 | Oh, little prince | _147 |

STEP 1. 원문 읽기 STEP 2. 구조 파악과 이해

| DAY 18 | On the fifth day | _153 |

STEP 1. 원문 읽기 STEP 2. 구조 파악과 이해

| DAY 19 | And you actually believe that the flowers | _159 |

STEP 1. 원문 읽기 STEP 2. 구조 파악과 이해

| DAY 20 | Is the warfare between the sheep and the flowers | _165 |

STEP 1. 원문 읽기 STEP 2. 구조 파악과 이해

| DAY 21 | STEP 3. 3주차 지문을 한 번에 읽어봐요 | _171 |

Week 4

DAY 22 **I soon learned to know this flower better** _185
STEP 1. 원문 읽기 STEP 2. 구조 파악과 이해

DAY 23 **But the little prince could not restrain** _191
STEP 1. 원문 읽기 STEP 2. 구조 파악과 이해

DAY 24 **But she interrupted herself at that point** _197
STEP 1. 원문 읽기 STEP 2. 구조 파악과 이해

DAY 25 **I believe that for his escape** _203
STEP 1. 원문 읽기 STEP 2. 구조 파악과 이해

DAY 26 **Of course I love you** _209
STEP 1. 원문 읽기 STEP 2. 구조 파악과 이해

DAY 27 **Approach, so that I may see you better** _215
STEP 1. 원문 읽기 STEP 2. 구조 파악과 이해

DAY 28 STEP 3. 4주차 지문을 한 번에 읽어봐요 _221

부록

앙투안 드 생텍쥐페리 _236

《어린 왕자》 _237

워밍업

1. '원서 읽기'란?

제가 처음 원서를 읽기 시작한 것, 정확히는 읽는 척을 시작한 건 '멋져 보였기 때문'이었습니다. 어느 날 지하철에서 원서를 읽는 사람이 눈에 들어왔는데 아주 멋져 보이더라고요. 그래서 저도 원서를 읽으려 시도했는데 너무 어려웠습니다.

그래서 밖에서는 보여주기 식으로 어려운 원서를 읽는 척을 하고, 혼자 있을 때는 여러 영어 학습법과, 쉬운 영어책을 보며 분석하고 연구했습니다. 300여권의 영어학습법과 200여권의 원서를 읽어보며 고민했지만 잘못된 영어 학습법으로 오염된 한국인에게 맞는 영어 독해법은 쉽게 찾아볼 수 없었습니다. 원어민들이나 해외파들은 그냥 많이 읽어보면 된다 하지만 해봐도 안 됐습니다.

어느 날 한참 서점을 노려보다가 아이디어가 떠올랐습니다. 그걸 적용해서 원서 독해법을 만들었습니다. 그리고 수년간 적용해봤습니다. 어려운 단어 뜻이나 문법을 몰라도 원서 읽기가 가능했습니다!

❶ 영어의 기본 5구조를 익히고,
❷ 영문장을 읽으면서 앞뒤로 왔다 갔다 하면서 '한국어로 번역'하지 말고,
❸ 5구조를 적용해서 그냥 순서대로 이해하면 됩니다.

한국인들은 워낙 영문을 읽고 '한국어 단어 뜻'을 일일이 생각해내고, '한국어로 깔끔히 번역'하는 학습법을 익혀왔기 때문에, 이렇게 영어 자체를 그대로 받아들이는데 꽤 많은 시간을 투자해서 연습해야 합니다.

책을 별로 안 읽는 사람이 보통 한국어 책을 1분에 300~500단어를 읽는다 합니다. (말하기 속도는 보통 분당 150~200단어) 그런데 한국 대학생들의 평균 영어 독해 속도는 약 70단어입니다. 이건 독서가 가능한 속도가 아니죠. 이렇게 속도가 느리니 영어를 들어서는 더욱 더 이해할 리가 없습니다. 이 책에서의 훈련 방법대로 연습하면서,

❶ 자기가 좋아하는 책을 '찾아.'
❷ 반복해서 읽어보세요.

그러면 분명히 속도가 나기 시작할 겁니다. 어느 순간 '내가 영어로 된 책을 읽고 있나?'라는 의식조차 없이 그냥 내용 자체를 이해하게 될 겁니다!

2. 영어의 5구조

학교에서 배운 5형식과는 다른 겁니다. 5형식은 몰라도 전혀 문제없고 오히려 방해됩니다.

1 주어 + 동사 (기본형)

일단 주어와 동사가 있어야 한 문장이 됩니다. 그런데 동사에 두 가지 형태가 있어요. 주어가 뭔가 행동하는 '→' 동사가 있고, 주어가 어떤 상태인지 '=' 상태를 나타내는 동사가 있습니다. 일반동사, be동사로 배워왔던 건데 여기선 →, = 로 설명할게요.

> I like you. / He studied english. 이런 건 → 가 쓰인 거고,
> I am tall. / She is pretty. 는 = 가 쓰인 겁니다.

그리고 우리가 자동사, 타동사로 무식하게 외워왔던 것 말인데요. 동사가 주어 스스로에게 영향 미치면 자동사, 뭔가 대상에게 영향을 미치면 타동사입니다. 말로 설명하는데 조금 한계가 있어요. 자꾸 자동사, 타동사 같은 문법 용어 나오면 저도 머리 아파져요. 항상 그냥 예문으로 익히는 게 좋아요. 자꾸 소리 내서 읽으며 영어 자체를 경험하면 돼요.

> 예1〉
>
> ㉧
> I go. (나는 간다. 가는 게 '나')

He swims. (수영하는 데 어떤 대상이 필요하진 않지요? ㄴ는 너를 수영해. X)

㉡

She likes you. (그녀가 좋아하는 대상이 'you')
They make computers. (그들이 만드는 것은 'computers')

경우에 따라 두 가지 역할을 하는 동사도 있어요.

예1)

I study this cafe. (나는 공부해 이 카페를) : 예를 들어 창업하려고 카페 연구 중일 때.

I study in this cafe. (나는 공부해 이 카페 안에서)
(한글 번역은 참고만 하고, 영어 자체 뉘앙스에 익숙해져야 돼요.)

예2)

Eat the cat. (먹어 그 고양이를) : 무섭(?)지만 자/타동사 이해를 위한 예문입니다.
Eat with the cat. (먹어 그 고양이랑 (같이)) : 보통 이런 식으로 쓰겠죠.

위의 예처럼 전치사 유무에 따라 두 가지 역할을 하는 동사도 있어요. 외우지 말고 예문을 소리 내서 읽어보세요. 누구한테 설명한다 치고 혼잣말로 설명해보는 것도 좋아요. 인형에게 '너 자동사랑 타동사가 뭔지 알아? 예시를 들어줄게~ eat the cat 하면 말야~' 이런 식으로요. ^^

이 책의 설명을 참고로, 많이 읽고 말해보면서 자연스레 익히면 됩니다. 일단 많이 '해'보고, 설명을 참고하는 겁니다. 우리는 설명만, 그것도 '잘못된' 설명을 '공부'만 했거든요.

PART 1 워밍업

2 전치사 + 명사

기본형에 명사를 데려올 땐 전치사를 쓰면 됩니다. 어떤 전치사를 쓰느냐가 문제인데요. 전치사라는 게 한국어에 없어서 그래요. 외국인들이 한국어를 배울 때 조사를 자주 빠뜨리는 것도 같은 이유입니다. ('미쿡싸람 풀고기 좋습니다!' 등등...) 어렵다기보다 그냥 새로운 걸 배운다고 생각하세요. ❶ 책의 설명을 참고하고, ❷ 자꾸 사용하며 시행착오 겪고, ❸ 다시 설명 참고해서 영어 원서 등을 통해 채워 넣으면 됩니다. 말하는 원서 편에 나누어서 설명해 놓았습니다.

- I go to school.   나는 간다 / 학교에
- I will run to you.   나는 달릴거야 / 너에게 (너 쪽으로)
- This book is for you.   이 책은 '=' 상태야 / 널 위한
- I wrote this book for you.   나는 썼다 이 책을 / 널 위해

3 to + 동사

기본형(주어+동사)에 동사를 더 데려올 땐 데려오는 동사 앞에 to를 둡니다. 이걸로 끝! to는 동사를 데려올 때도, 명사를 데려올 때도 쓸 수 있어요. 뒤에서 to에 대해 더 설명하겠지만, to 부정사니 이런 어려운 말은 몰라도 되고 to가 나오면 '방향' '그 쪽으로 움직이려 함' 정도의 느낌을 일단 잡아두면 됩니다.

- I go to study. 나는 간다 / 공부하려고
- He has a book to read. 그는 가졌다 한 책을 / 읽을 or 읽으려고
- He sings to meet you. 그는 노래한다 / 만나려고 너를
- This book is to guide you. 이 책은 '=' 상태다 / 이끌려고 너를

> 직접 만들어 볼까요?
>
> • 나는 (한) 선생님이야 / 가르칠 너를
>   : _____
>
> • 나는 공부해 / 가려고 미국에
>   : _____
>
> • 나는 원해 / 말하기를 영어를
>   : _____
>
> • 그는 원해 / 오기를 여기에
>   : _____

4 분사(동사 변형)

분사도 되게 어렵게 배워왔는데 간단히 알려 드릴게요.
❶ 한 문장에 동사가 이미 있는데 또 하나의 동작이 있으면 동사를 변형해서 붙입니다.
❷ 동사를 변형시켜서 명사를 꾸미는 용도로 사용할 수 있어요. 무슨 말이냐고요?

쉬운 설명 나갑니다!

프라이드치킨이라고 하죠? 프라이팬이라고 하고요. 이거 사실 fried chicken이고 frying pan이에요. 기본 동사 fry(튀기다. 튀겨라)가 fried 아님 frying 형태로 변형되는데 -ed 형태가 되면 '~된 거'이고 -ing 형태면 '~하는 것'이 돼요. 그래서 우리말로 설명하자면 fried chicken은 '튀겨진' chicken이 되고 frying pan는 '튀기는' pan이 돼요.

여기서 중요한건 동사와 분사의 뜻을 일일이 외우는 게 아니라 영어를 접하다가 fried chicken이란 게 나오면 '아... fry 뜻은 내가 모르지만 암튼 이건 fry가 된 치킨이란 소리구나' 이걸 알 수 있단 거고 알아야 한단 거죠. 잘 이해 안 되면 일단 넘어가고 다음에 다시 보세요!

5 접속사

접속사에는 두 가지가 있어요. 한 가지는 and, but, when 이런 접속사예요. 이런 접속사를 '등위접속사'라고 부르는 것은 몰라도 됩니다. (저도 책 쓴다고 찾아봤어요.) 암튼 이런 접속사는 한 문장에 다른 문장을 데려올 수 있습니다.

> I like you and you like him. (슬프군요. ^^)
> You read books when I watch TV.

다른 한 가지가 관계대명사라는 건데, 좀 많이 연습해야 돼요. 한국어와 어순에서 차이가 있기 때문인데요. 역시 자세한 문법은 몰라도 되고, 말문 트기 편에서 상세히 익힐 수 있어요.

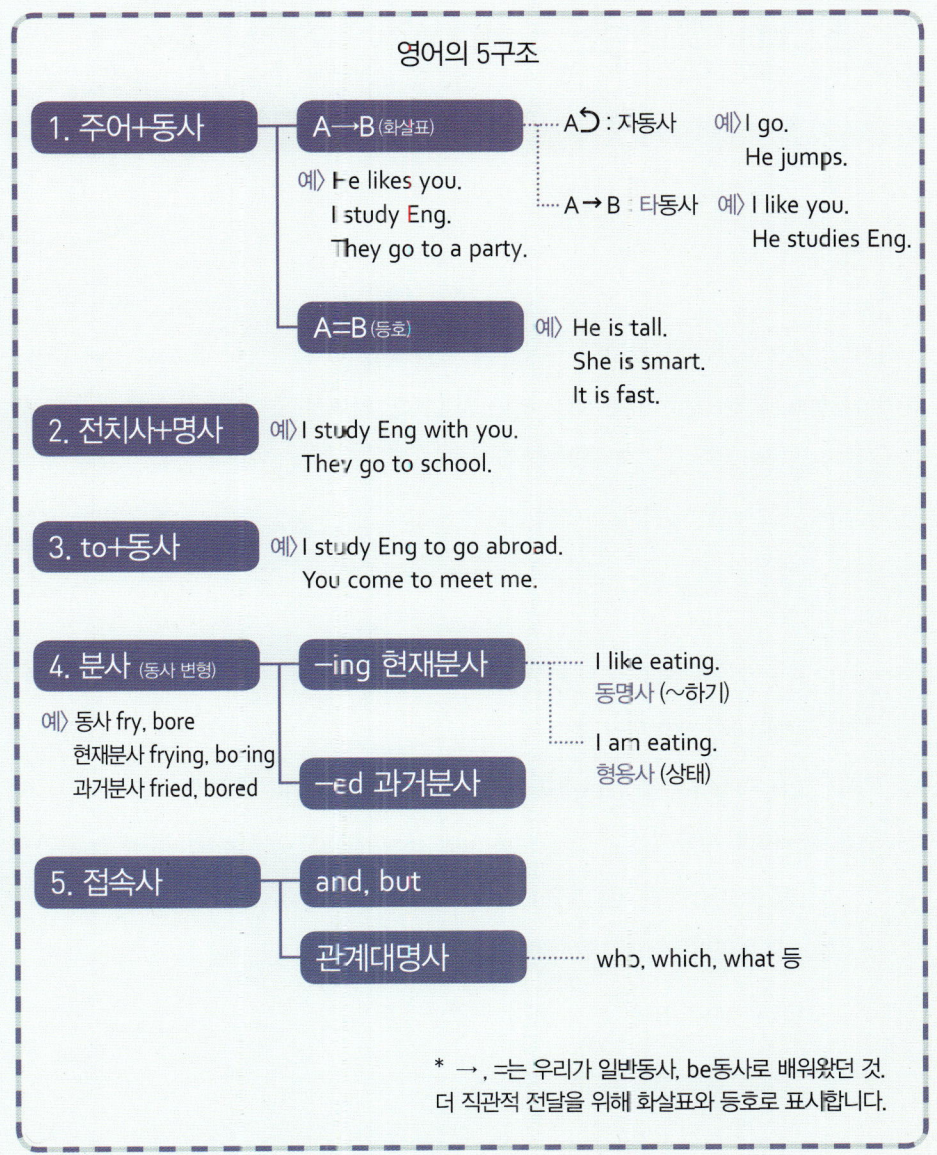

3. 문법 공부는 이제 그만!

우리도 한국어 문법 잘 모릅니다. 그래도 한국어 쓰는 데 불편함이 없죠. (일본에서 한국의 영어 교육을 망쳐놨어요.) 운전 배울 때와 비교하면 돼요. 빨간불, 파란불의 의미를 알고 액셀과 브레이크의 구분 정도의 실제 운전에 필요한 것들만 알고 몸에 익히면 운전이 가능하죠. 그래서 이 책에선 어려우면서 필요도 없는 문법들을 다 뺐습니다. 정말 최소한의 용어들만 남겼다고 보면 돼요. (용어는 이름, 명칭이라 어찌 할 수가 없네요.)

- 주어 : 무대의 배우라고 보면 돼요.
- 동사 : 그 배우가 하는 동작 (be동사라고 해서 동작이 없을 수도 있어요.)
- 부사 : 동사의 동작을 꾸며 줍니다. 보통 뒤에 -ly가 붙어요. 부사는 없어도 문장 구조엔 별 영향을 안 끼쳐요. (I will live peacefully. / He thinks deeply.)
- 명사 : 이름이에요!! 명식이, 호식이, 호랑이, 지우개, 연필 등... 좀 더 알고 싶다면 《Basic Grammar in Use》란 책을 읽어보세요.

이 책에서 꼭 알아야 하는 건 주어와 동사입니다. 이게 기본 문장을 만들거든요! 기본 주어, 동사가 무엇인지 파악이 돼야 영어 독해, 독서를 제대로 할 수 있어요. 동사를 못 찾으면 엉뚱하게 이해하게 됩니다. 영어 단어 수천 개 이상을 알면서도 원서를 이해 못하게 돼요. 훈련 코스에서 계속 따로 표시해 둘 거예요.

문법은 원래 안 해도 되는 것! (EBS 역사 채널 내용 중!)

1882년 조미수호통상조약(조선과 미국이 문화와 학술을 교류한다는 내용의 조약) 후 방미사절단 일행이 전해온 새로운 문화에 감탄한 고종 임금님이 영어 교육의 필요성을 느끼고 왕립영어학교를 설치하여 한국인들이 영어를 잘 배우게 되었습니다. 같은 시기 선교사들이 세운 학교에서도 원어민과 영어로 대화하면서 그들의 문화를 배우는 방식을 통해 출세를 꿈꾸는 많은 이들이 영어를 열심히 익혔다 해요. 영국 영사에서도 조선이 동양에서 가장 어학에 뛰어나 중국이나 일본이 감히 따르지 못할 것이라 본국에 보고했을 정도입니다. 그런데 1905년 을사조약이 체결되고, 일제가 교육 제도를 개편했어요. 일본인 교사들은 영어를 일본어로 번역하고 문법을 가르쳤습니다. 그로 인해 조선인들의 어학 실력은 망가지기 시작했죠. 그 당시 일제 강점기 교육법이 독립 이후까지 이어져 한국인들의 벙어리 영어를 만드는 데 결정적 역할을 했습니다. 조금씩 바뀌고는 있지만 여전히 많은 분들이 문법을 해야 되냐 묻고, 문법 강의를 많은 곳에서 합니다. 위 내용을 보면 알겠지만, 안 해도 됩니다. 일본식 교육의 폐해입니다.

4. 직관적 리딩

I caught a gleam of light in the impenetrable mystery of his presence.

이런 문장을 보면 '어렵다' 할 수 있잖아요? 그런데 구조를 보면, 이런 식입니다.

I caught a gleam
        of light
                in the impenetrable mystery
                        of his presence.

좀 복잡한 단어의 첫 글자를 약자로 잡아 정리하면,

I caught a gleam of light in the impenetrable mystery of his presence.
I C   a G   of L   in   M of P

쉬운 단어로 바꾸면,

I caught a cat of yours in the house of yours.
같은 형태지요.

이런 식으로 최대한 직관적으로 한국어 없이, 보면 이해될 수 있는 장치들을 넣었어요. 다른 문장으로 한 번 더 설명할게요. 아무리 긴 영문장이라도 결국 (1) 주어+동사(기본형)에 (2) 전치사+명사 (3) to+동사 (4) 분사(동사 변형) (5) 접속사가 붙어 영문장이 만들어(길어)집니다. (영어의 5구조)

I go.

I go to gym. (3)

I go to gym with my dog. (3, 2)

I go to gym with my dog to exercise. (3, 2, 3)

I go to gym with my dog which can run to exercise with me. (3, 2, 5, 3, 2)

조금 모양을 바꿔보면, 이런 식이 돼요.

I go

　　to gym (3)

　　　　with my dog (2)

　　　　　　which can run (5)

　　　　　　　　to exercise (3)

　　　　　　　　　　with me. (2)

영문장을 보고 앞뒤로 왔다 갔다 하며 한국어로 '번역'을 해서는 영문장을 제대로 이해할 수 없게 됩니다. 절대 위 문장을 보고 '나는 달리기를 할 수 있는 강아지와 운동을 하러...' 이렇게 하지 말라는 거예요. 그냥 적힌 순서대로 영어를 이해해야 돼요.

5. 원서 읽기 FAQ

1. 추천 원서를 알려 주세요

본인이 읽고 싶은 책을 '찾.으.세.요.' 물론 기본적으로 추천할 책이야 있지만 결국 자기가 재밌어야 읽습니다. 그러려면 본인이 서점, 도서관에 가서 직접 페이지 펼쳐보고 읽어보면서 찾아야 합니다. 이왕이면 쉽고 유익한 책이면 좋겠습니다만, 가장 중요한 것은 '자기가 읽고 싶은 책'을 찾.는.것.입니다. 이것을 알려주는 책이 없어서 저도 시행착오를 여러 번 겪었습니다. 자기가 좋아하는 분야에 대한 책을 원서로 읽어보세요. 자기가 무엇을 좋아하는지 모른다면, 관심 분야를 빨리 찾아야 하겠고요. 국내 도서도 한 달에 1~2권 읽지 않는 사람은 일단 독서 습관부터 길러야 합니다. 원래 책을 안 읽는 사람이, 영어로 된 책을 읽기는 너무 힘듭니다.

굳이 추천 도서를 알려 드리자면, 일단 난이도별로 나와 있는 책들이 있습니다. 난이도 별로 쉬운 책부터 읽어나가면 좋아요. 쉬운 것부터 확실히 해나가면 좋겠어요. 토익 고득점자도 1단계 레벨조차 제대로 못 읽는 분 많습니다. 그 외에도, 분량이 많지 않거나, 챕터별로 나뉘어 있는 책들 중에 좋은 것을 찾을 수 있을 겁니다.

2. 모르는 단어는 어떻게?

원서를 읽는 것도 '독서'입니다. 다만 언어가 '영어'라는 점이 다를 뿐입니다만, 많은 분들이 '공부'로 생각하고 자꾸 분석하고, 밑줄 치고, 암기합니다. 국내 드서나, 신문 읽을 때를 생각해보세요. 큰 흐름만 이해하면 넘어가지, 일일이 단어 하나하나 분석하는 사람은 없을 겁니다. 그건 '국어 공부'지 '독서'가 아니죠. 같은 맥락으로 원서를 읽을 때도, 흐름을 이해하는 데 큰 무리가 없으면 적당히 넘어가면 됩니다. 그런 식으로 꾸준히 영어를 접하면, 자연스럽게 '영어 자체'를 이해하게 됩니다.

절대로 영단어와 우리말을 일대일 대응시키려고 하지 마세요. 원서를 읽으면서 자꾸 사전을 찾아보면 영어 자체로 읽는 흐름이 끊깁니다. 원서를 읽는 것도 아닌, 한국어 단어 공부도 아닌 그야말로 이도저도 아닌 게 됩니다. 모르는 단어가 너무 많을 경우엔 난이도를 조금 낮추는 것도 좋겠습니다. 단어에 관한 부분은 '자기가 정말 읽고 싶은 책'을 찾게 되면 자연스럽게 해결되는 부분이라고도 말할 수 있습니다.

3. 단어 뜻을 정확히 알고 싶어요?!

한국어로 어설픈 번역하는 학습법을 해와서 생기는 문제인데요. 단어 뜻을 '정확히' 알려달라는 질문이 많아요. 여기서 말하는 '정확'은 '한국어로 깔끔히'를 주로 말하더라고요. 계속 말하지만 '한국어로 깔끔히' 답을 드릴수록 점점 영어와는 멀어지게 됩니다. 영어책을 읽었는데 왜 머릿속에 한국어가 남아야 하나요.

결국에는 영영사전을 봐야 되는데, 처음에는 어려우니 이 책을 통해 영어 독해에 익숙해질 때까진 영한사전을 참고하면 됩니다. 해서 대략의 뜻을 한국어로 익히다가, 영어 독해가 느는 시점을 잘 파악해서 영영사전으로 꼭 넘어가세요. 영어 자체의 뉘앙스를 파악하게 되어 영어가 많이 늘 거예요.

4. 해석이 안 돼요

정확하게는 한국어로 '깔끔한 번역'이 안 돼서 답답함을 느끼는 겁니다. 번역은 번역가가 하는 거고 우리는 적혀있는 영문만 이해하면 되는데, 문장을 분석하고 의역하는 공부법으로 배워와서 방해받는 겁니다. 흐름에 지장을 주는 정도가 아니라면 그냥 넘어가세요. 읽고 나서 머릿속에 어떤 이미지가 남으면 됩니다. (이 부분이 중요!! 이게 쌓이는 것이 진짜 영어 INPUT이 남은 겁니다.) 우리말로 바뀐 문장들이 남아있으면 안 됩니다. 만약 전혀 흐름을 파악할 수 없다면, 조금 쉬운 단계의 책을 읽는 것도 좋겠습니다.

❶ 보통 한국인은(중고등학교에서 영어를 잘못 배운!) 영어를 읽으면 답답하다고 느낍니다. 그 답답함을 버텨내야 영어뇌가 활성화 되는데 말이에요.

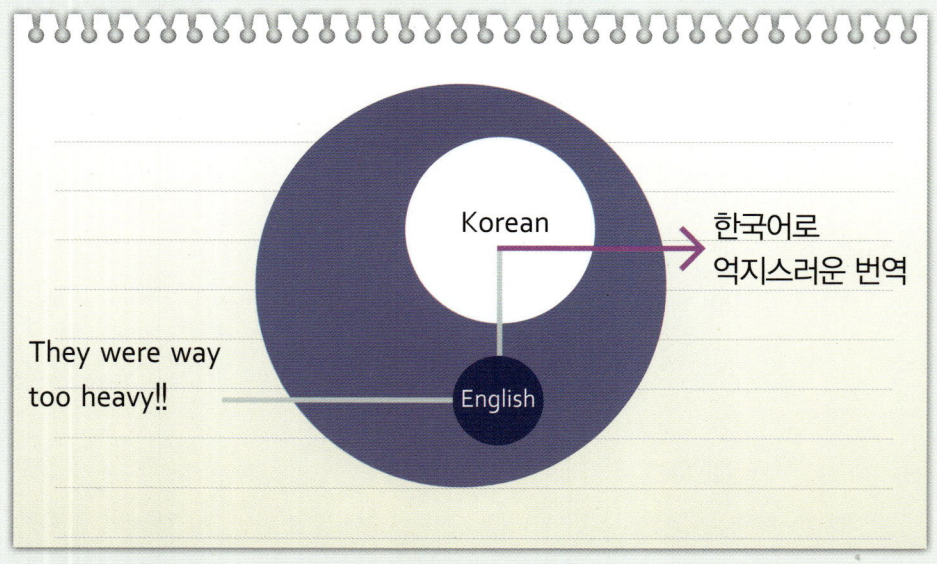

❷ 원서를 소리 내어 반복해서 읽으면, 한국어로 번역할 여유가 없이 계속 영어를 읽고 말하게 되므로 영어방이 활성화되기 시작합니다.

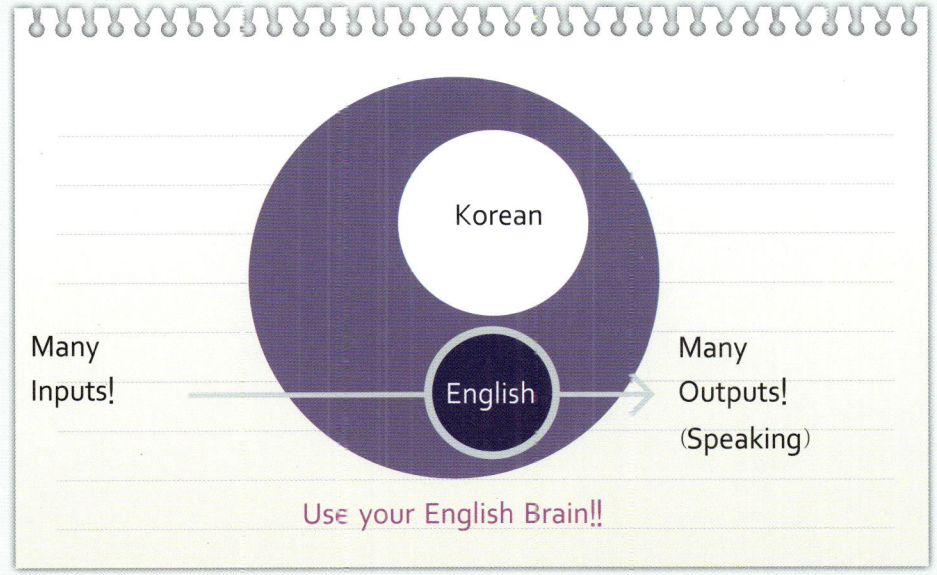

❸ 이 작업이 일정량을 넘기게 되면 영어방이 확장되어 영어를 영어 자체로 이해하게 됩니다.

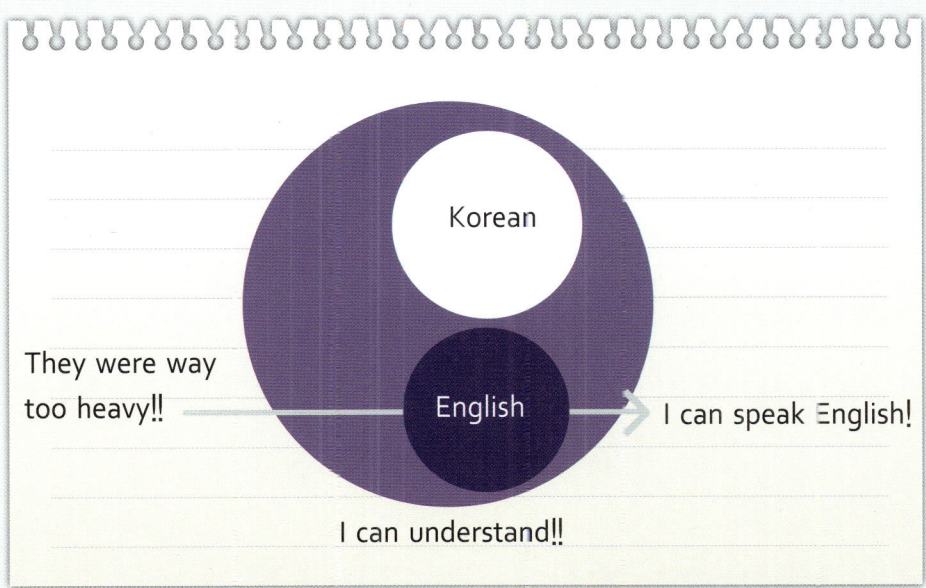

5. 우리말로 번역하지 말라는데, 잘 안 돼요

한국의 성인들은 10년 이상 영어를 한국어로 어설프게 번역하는 연습을 해왔습니다. 정말로 심각한 문제 중에 하나이고 쉽게 고칠 수 없는 부분이기도 하죠. 다음과 같은 방법으로 읽어보세요.

❶ 소리 내어 읽는다.

소리를 내게 되면, 소리에 신경 쓰느라 한국어로 번역할 여유가 없을 겁니다. 이게 반복되면 자연스럽게 영어 자체의 뉘앙스들이 쌓이게 됩니다. 그러면서 영어 자체로 받아들일 수 있게 되죠. 모든 영어 공부법 책들과 모든 영어 선생님들이 쉬운 원서를 반복해서 소리 내서 읽으라는 이유가 여기에 있습니다.

❷ 시간을 설정하고 읽는다.

그냥 편하게 읽으면 자꾸 우리말로 번역하고, 딴 생각을 하게 됩니다. '10분 동안 5페이지를 읽는다!' 식의 구체적 목표를 설정하고, 절대로 되돌아가지 말고, 쭉쭉 눈으로만 확인하는 느낌으로 읽어보세요. 번역할 여유를 주지 마세요. 점점 영어 자체가 남게 될 겁니다.

6. 페이지가 안 넘어가요

제가 지하철이나 카페에서 원서를 많이 읽으라고 권해드리면, 페이지가 안 넘어가서 창피하단 분이 많습니다. 간단합니다. 그냥 가끔씩 페이지를 넘겨주면 됩니다. ^^ 제가 좋아하는 말 중에 '진짜가 될 때까지 진짜인 척하라'라는 말이 있습니다. 위에서 조언해 드린 부분을 참고하면, 몇 달 안에 제대로 된 독해를 시작하게 될 겁니다.

7. 원서 읽기도 결국 책 읽기!

많은 분들(처음의 저 포함)이 오해하거나, 생각 못하는 게 원서 읽기도 결국 책 읽기란 겁니다. 영어 '공부'라고 생각한 나머지 모르는 단어가 나올 때마다 일일이 사전 찾아보고, 밑줄 치고, 분석하다가 한 장을 제대로 못 넘기는 경우가 많았을 거예요. 물론 한국인들이 원서 읽기를 해 오지 않고, 문법 위주로 독해를 하는 바람에 거기서 벗어나고, 고치는 작업이 필요하긴 해요. 그래서 원문과 한국어 번역본을 한 줄씩 비교해 가며 '공부'하는 작업이 필요한 시점이 있기도 합니다. 그런데 결국, 어쨌거나 원서 읽기도 '책 읽기'입니다. 책을 별로 안 읽는 사람이 원서를 읽기는 쉽지 않아요. 원서라 해서 읽었는데, 이해 안 되는 것은 영어 문제만이 아닐 수 있어요. (배경지식이 부족하거나, 이해력이 부족하거나, 아니면 작가가 글을 난해하게 썼거나) 영어 학습에 있어 두 가지 인풋 경로가 ❶ 읽기, ❷ 듣기일 텐데요. 듣기 방법이 계속 연구되고 있지만 아직 쉽지 않은 만큼, 또한 읽기도 되지 않는데 듣기(귀로 하는 읽기이므로)가 될 리가 없는 만큼 '원서 읽기' 능력은 아주 중요합니다. 점점 영어 중요성이 더 커지고 있기도 하고요. 영어 학습법 전문가 전에 이미 독서법 전문가로 알려진 제가 독서에 대한 팁을 여기서도 정리해 보면요.

세상에 살면서 배움의 방법이 ❶ 사람, ❷ 강의, ❸ 책 이렇게 세 가지가 있는데요. 사람을 일일이 만나 배울 수 있으면 그게 최고 좋겠지만 여러 제약들이 있잖아요(장소, 비용, 시간 등). 그런데 책은 그런 제약을 뛰어넘게 해주죠. 반복해서 이야기를 접할 수 있고, 정리도 잘 되어 있지요. 그래서 책이 좋은 거 같아요. 책을 어렵게 생각하는 분이 있는데, 책은 결국 '어떤 사람이 쓴' '긴 편지'거든요. 이 책도 마찬가지고요. 제가 여러분을 일일이 만나서 영어로 된 책을 읽는 법에 대해 상세히, 꾸준히 알려드리기가 쉽지 않잖아요? 그래서 그 방법을 상세히 열심히 작업해서 이렇게 긴 편지로 남기는 겁니다. 여러분을 아끼는 마음으로 이 편지를 쓰고 있는 거예요. 모르는 이라 생각지 마세요. ^^ 그럼 더 도움 되기도 하고, 반가울 거잖아요.

PART 2

원서 읽기 훈련 코스
: 《어린 왕자》

- 아름다운 이야기 《어린 왕자》 원서 읽기에 도전해봅시다. 영어의 기본 5구조를 익히고, 영문장을 읽으면서 앞뒤로 왔다 갔다 하면서 '한국어로 번역'하지 말고, 5구조를 적용해서 그냥 순서대로 이해하면 됩니다.

- 10~20개의 단어, 4~6개 정도의 5구조로 구성된 문장들로 훈련합니다. 한 주의 학습 분량은 Step 1 원문 읽기, Step 2 구조 파악과 이해(5구조 분석), Step 3 길주일 분량의 원문 한 번에 읽어보기 순서로 진행됩니다.

WEEK 1

이 책에서 꼭 알아야 하는 건 주어와 동사입니다. 이게 기본 문장을 만들거든요! 기본 주어, 동사가 무엇인지 파악이 돼야 영어 독해, 독서를 제대로 할 수 있어요. 동사를 못 찾으면 엉뚱하게 이해하게 됩니다.

Step 1 원문 읽기

Once when I was six years old I saw a magnificent picture in a book.¹ It was called *True Stories from Nature*, about the primeval forest.² It was a picture of a boa constrictor in the act of swallowing an animal.³ Here is a copy of the drawing.⁴

In the book it said: "Boa constrictors swallow their prey whole, without chewing it.⁵ After that they are not able to move, and they sleep through the six months that they need for digestion."

I pondered deeply, then, over the adventures of the jungle. And after some work with a colored pencil I succeeded in making my first drawing.⁶ My Drawing Number One. It looked like this:

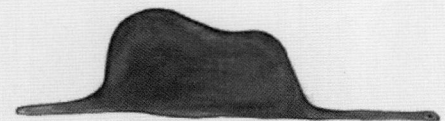

I showed my masterpiece to the grown-ups, and asked them whether the drawing frightened them.⁷ But they answered: "Frighten? Why should any one be frightened by a hat?"⁸

Step 1 원문 읽기

My drawing was not a picture of a hat. It was a picture of a boa constrictor digesting an elephant.⁹ But since the grown-ups were not able to understand it, I made another drawing: I drew the inside of the boa constrictor, so that the grown-ups could see it clearly.¹⁰

They always need to have things explained.¹¹ My Drawing Number Two looked like this:

---

1. When I was S, I saw P, in a B.
2. It was called T from N about F. 'primeval' 이런 단어 뜻 일일이 찾지 마세요. 구조 위주로 보고, 문장 안에서 guess!!
3. It was P of B in A of S–ing
4. Here is A of B ing n C.
5. A swallow B without C–ing. = A → B without C–ing.
6. And after A with B, I succeeded in C–ing D.
7. whether I liked you와 같은 형태.
8. Why should A be tired?와 같은 형태.
9. It was A of B C–ing B.
10. the grown-ups : grow–grew–grown에서 grown은 '자란' 정도의 분사잖아요. 형용사 앞에 the가 붙으면 그런 '~들'이 돼요. 그래서 '어른들'이란 뜻이 됩니다.
11. They A to B C D–ed. explained는 동사가 아님!

Step 2 구조 파악과 이해

01. Once when I was six years old(5)
　　　　　I saw a magnificent picture
　　　　　　　　　　in a book.(2)

02. It was called *True Stories*
　　　　from Nature,(2)
　　　　　about the primeval forest.(2)

03. It was a picture
　　　of a boa constrictor(2)
　　　　in the act(2)
　　　　　of swallowing an animal.(2, 4)

04. Here is a copy
　　　of the drawing.(2)
　　In the book(2)
　　　it said:

05. "Boa constrictors swallow their prey whole,
　　　　　without chewing it.(2)

06. After that
　　　they are not able
　　　　to move,(3)

07. and they sleep
　　　through the six months(2)
　　　　that they need(5)
　　　　　for digestion."(2)

Step 2 구조 파악과 이해

08. I pondered deeply, then,
   over the adventures(2)
   of the jungle.(2)

09. And after some work(2)
   with a colored pencil(2, 4)
   I succeeded
   in making my first drawing.(2)

10. My Drawing Number One. It looked
   like this:(2)

11. I showed my masterpiece
   to the grown-ups,(2, 4)

12. and asked them
   whether the drawing frightened them.(5)

13. But they answered: "Frighten?
   Why should any one be frightened(4)
   by a hat?"(2)

14. My drawing was not a picture
   of a hat.(2)

15. It was a picture
   of a boa constrictor(2)
   digesting an elephant.(4)

16. But since the grown-ups were not able
   to understand it,(3)

Step 2 구조 파악과 이해

I made another drawing:
17. I drew the inside
　　　of the boa constrictor,(2)
　　　　　so that the grown-ups could see it clearly.(5)
18. They always need
　　　to have things(3)
　　　　explained.(4)
19. My Drawing Number Two looked
　　　　　like this:(2)

DAY2

Step 1 원문 읽기

The grown-ups' response, this time, was to advise me to lay aside my drawings.[1] They said: "Don't draw boa constrictors, whether from the inside or the outside and devote[2] yourself instead to geography, history, arithmetic, and grammar."

That is why, at the age of six, I gave up to be a magnificent career as a painter. I had been disheartened by the failure of my Drawing Number One and Two. Grown-ups never understand anything by themselves, and it is tiresome for children to be always and forever explaining things to them.

So then I chose another profession, and learned to pilot airplanes. I have flown a little over all parts of the world; and it is true that geography has been very useful to me. At a glance I can distinguish China from Arizona. If one gets lost in the night, such knowledge is valuable.

In the course of this life I have had a great many encounters with a many people. They have been concerned with matters of consequence.

I have lived a great deal among grown-ups. I have seen them intimately, close at hand. And that hasn't much improved my opinion of them.

Step 1 원문 읽기

Whenever I met one of them who seemed to me at all clear-sighted, I tried the experiment of showing him my Drawing Number One, which I have always kept.[3] I would try to find out, so, if this was a person of true understanding. But, whoever it was, he, or she, would always say:

"That is a hat."

---

1. response was(1) to advise.
2. 동사원형이 맨 앞에 나오면 명령어(주어 you 생략).
3. 진짜 주어+동사 I tried 다음을 줄이면 다음과 같은 모양이 됩니다. I tried E of S-ing him D N O which I have.

Step 2 구조 파악과 이해

01. The grown-ups' response, this time, was
                to advise me(3)
                to lay aside my drawings.(3)

02. They said:
        "Don't draw boa constrictors,
            whether from the inside or the outside(5)

03. and devote yourself instead
    to geography,
        history, arithmetic, and grammar."(2)

04. That is why,
      at the age(2)
        of six,(2)
          I gave up(5)
            to be a magnificent career(3)
              as a painter.(2)

05. I had been disheartened
      by the failure(2)
        of my Drawing Number One and Two.(2)

06. Grown-ups never understand anything
        by themselves,(2)

07. and it is tiresome
    for children(2)
      to be always and forever explaining(3)

Step 2 구조 파악과 이해

                          things

                              to them.(2)

8. So then I chose another profession,

            and learned

                  to pilot airplanes.(3)

9. I have flown a little

                over all parts(2)

                  of the world;(2)

10. and it is true

        that geography has been very useful(3)

                        to me.(2)

11. At a glance(2)

    I can distinguish China

              from Arizona.(2)

12. If one gets lost(5)

      in the night,(2)

        such knowledge is valuable.

13. In the course(2)

      of this life(2)

          I have had a great many encounters

                  with a many people.(2)

14. They have been concerned

        with matters(2)

Step 2 구조 파악과 이해

        of consequence.(2)

15. I have lived a great deal

        among grown-ups.(2)

16. I have seen them intimately, close

        at hand.(2)

17. And that hasn't much improved my opinion

        of them.(2)

18. Whenever I met one(5)

        of them(2)

        who seemed to me(5, 2)

        at all clear-sighted,(2)

19. I tried the experiment

        of showing him(2, 4)

        my Drawing Number One,

        which I have always kept.(5)

20. I would try

        to find out, so,(3)

21. if this was a person(5)

        of true understanding.(2)

22. But, whoever it was,(5)

        he, or she, would always say:

23. "That is a hat."

DAY 3

Step 1 원문 읽기

Then I would never talk to that person about boa constrictors, or primeval forests, or stars. I would bring myself down to his level.

I would talk to him about bridge, and golf, and politics, and neckties.
And the grown-up would be greatly pleased to have met such a sensible man.

So I lived my life alone, without anyone that I could really talk to, until I had an accident with my plane in the Desert of Sahara, six years ago.

Something was broken in my engine. And as I had with me neither a mechanic nor any passengers, I set myself to attempt the difficult repairs all alone. It was a question of life or death for me: I had scarcely enough drinking water to last a week.

The first night, then, I went to sleep on the sand, a thousand miles from any human habitation. I was more isolated than a shipwrecked sailor on a raft in the middle of the ocean.

Thus you can imagine my amazement, at sunrise, when I was awakened by an odd little voice. It said:

Step 1 원문 읽기

"If you please — draw me a sheep!"
"What!"
"Draw me a sheep!"

I jumped to my feet, completely thunderstruck. I blinked my eyes hard. I looked carefully all around me.

읽고 나서 머릿속에 한국거가 남으면 안돼요. 스토리의 이미지, 흐름이 남아야 합니다.

Step 2 구조 파악과 이해

01. Then I would never talk
    to that person(2)
        about boa constrictors,(2)
            or primeval forests, or stars.

02. I would bring myself down
        to his level.(2)

03. I would talk
    to him(2)
        about bridge,(2)
            and golf, and politics, and neckties.

04. And the grown-up would be
    greatly pleased(4)
        to have met such a sensible man.(3)

05. So I lived my life alone,
    without anyone(2)
        that I could really talk to,(5, 2)

06. until I had an accident(5)
    with my plane(2)
        in the Desert(2)
            of Sahara,(2)
                six years ago.

07. Something was broken(4)
    in my engine.(2)

Step 2 구조 파악과 이해

08. And as I had(5)

    with me(2)

        neither a mechanic nor any passengers,(2)

09. I set myself

    to attempt(3)

        the difficult repairs all alone.

10. It was a question

    of life or death for me:(2)

11. I had scarcely enough drinking water(4)

        to last a week.(2)

12. The first night, then, I went

    to sleep(3)

        on the sand, a thousand miles(2)

            from any human habitation.(2)

13. I was more isolated(4)

    than a shipwrecked sailor(2)

    on a raft(2)

        in the middle(2)

            of the ocean.(2)

14. Thus you can imagine my amazement,

    at sunrise,(2)

15. when I was awakened(5)

    by an odd little voice.(2)

Step 2 구조 파악과 이해

It said:

16. "If you please – draw me a sheep!"

17. "What!"

"Draw me a sheep!"

18. I jumped
    to my feet,(2)
        completely
            thunderstruck.(4)

19. I blinked my eyes hard.
      I looked carefully all
          around me.(2)

And I saw a most extraordinary small person, who stood there examining me with great seriousness. Here you may see the best portrait that, later, I was able to make of him. But my drawing is certainly very much less charming than its model.

That, however, is not my fault. The grown-ups discouraged me in my painter's career when I was six years old, and I never learned to draw anything, except boas from the outside and boas from the inside.

Now I stared at this sudden apparition with my eyes fairly starting out of my head in astonishment. Remember, I had crashed in the desert a thousand miles from any inhabited region.[1]

And yet my little man seemed neither to be straying uncertainly among the sands, nor to be fainting from fatigue or hunger or thirst or fear.

Step 1 원문 읽기

Nothing about him gave any suggestion of a child lost in the middle of the desert, a thousand miles from any human habitation. When at last I was able to speak, I said to him:

"But – what are you doing here?"

And in answer he repeated, very slowly, as if he were speaking of a matter of great consequence:

"If you please – draw me a sheep..."

---
1. Remember가 이 문장의 기본 뼈대(명령어)입니다.

Step 2 구조 파악과 이해

01. And I saw
　　　a most extraordinary small person,
　　　　　who stood there(5)
　　　　　　examining me(4)
　　　　　　　with great seriousness.(2)
02. Here you may see the best portrait
　　　　that, later, I was able(5)
　　　　　to make(3)
　　　　　　of him.(2)
03. But my drawing is certainly
　　　very much less charming(4)
　　　　than its model.(5)
04. That, however, is not my fault.
05. The grown-ups discouraged me
　　　in my painter's career(2)
　　　　when I was six years old,(5)
06. and I never learned
　　　to draw anything,(3)
　　　　except boas(2)
　　　　　from the outside and boas(2)
　　　　　　from the inside.(2)
07. Now I stared
　　　at this sudden apparition(2)

Step 2 구조 파악과 이해

with my eyes fairly(2)

starting out(4)

of my head(2)

in astonishment.(2)

08. Remember,

I had crashed

in the desert a thousand miles(2)

from any inhabited region.(2)

09. And yet my little **man seemed** neither

to be straying uncertainly(3, 4)

among the sands,(2)

10. nor to be fainting(3, 4)

from fatigue

or hunger or thirst or fear.(2)

11. Nothing

about him(2)

gave any suggestion

of a child(2)

lost(4)

in the middle(2)

of the desert,(2)

12. a thousand miles

from any human habitation.(2)

Step 2 구조 파악과 이해

13. When at last(5)
　　　　I was able
　　　　　　to speak, I said(3)
　　　　　　　　to him:(2)
14. "But —what are you doing here?"
15. And in answer(2)
　　　　he repeated, very slowly,
16. as if he were speaking(5)
　　　　of a matter(2)
　　　　　　of great consequence:(2)
17. "If you please —draw me a sheep..."(5)

DAY 5

Step 1 원문 읽기

When a mystery is too overpowering, one dare not disobey.[1] Absurd as it might seem to me, a thousand miles from any human habitation and in danger of death,[2] I took out of my pocket a sheet of paper and my fountain-pen. Then I remembered how my studies had been concentrated on geography, history, and grammar, and I told the little chap that I did not know how to draw. He answered me:

"That doesn't matter. Draw me a sheep..."

But I had never drawn a sheep. So I drew for him one of the two pictures I had drawn so often. It was that of the boa constrictor from the outside. And I was astounded to hear the little fellow greet it with,[3]

"No, no, no! I do not want an elephant inside a boa constrictor. A boa constrictor is a very dangerous creature, and an elephant is very cumbersome.[4] Where I live, everything is very small. What I need is a sheep.[5] Draw me a sheep."

So then I made a drawing.

He looked at it carefully, then he said:

Step 1 원문 읽기

"No. This sheep is already very sickly. Make me another."

So I made another drawing.

My friend smiled gently and indulgently.

"You see yourself," he said, "that this is not a sheep. This is a ram. It has horns."

So then I did my drawing over once more.

어린 왕자가 말을 짧게 해서... 쉬울 수도 있고, 조금 난해할 수도 있어요.
1. dare는 한국어에 대응시키기 많이 애매한 단어예요. 일단은 '감히' 정도로 보고, 특히 그냥 영문 자체로 많이 접해야 돼요. one dare not (to) disobey 식으로 동사를 데려오는 to가 생략된 형태.
2. 동사가 없네요. 그냥 명사로 설명만 하고 있는 문장입니다.
3. to hear the fellow (to) greet이 원형. 지각동사도 뒤에 데려오는 to를 자주 생략해요.
4. cumbersome의 뜻을 한국어 정확히 몰라도 구조 파악하는 더 문제없으니 그냥 문장 안에서 추측하거나, 궁금하면 사전 검색. '크끼리는 매우 구종한 동물입니다'라는 문장에서 '구종'을 모른다고 한국어를 못하는 게 아닌 것과 같아요. 그냥 그 단어 뜻을 모르는 것일 뿐. ('구종'은 제가 임의로 만든 단어)
5. What is a sheep이 기본 뼈대.

Step 2 구조 파악과 이해

01. When a mystery is too overpowering,(5)
   　　　　　　　　　　one **dare** not disobey.
02. Absurd as it might seem to me,
03. a thousand miles
   　　　　from any human habitation(2)
   　　　　　　　　and in danger(5, 2)
   　　　　　　　　　　　　of death,(2)
04. I took out
   　　　　of my pocket a sheet(2)
   　　　　　　　　of paper and my fountain-pen.(2)
05. Then I remembered
   　　　　how my studies had been(5)
   　　　　　　　　concentrated
   　　　　　　　　　　　　on geography, history, and grammar,(2)
06. and I told the little chap
   　　　　that I did not know(5)
   　　　　　　　　how to draw.(5)
07. He answered me:
   　　　　"That doesn't matter.
   　　　　　　　　Draw me a sheep…"
08. But I had never drawn a sheep.
09. So I drew
   　　　　for him one(2)

Step 2 구조 파악과 이해

        of the two pictures(2)

          (that) I had drawn so often.(5)

10. It was that

    of the boa constrictor(2)

      from the outside.(2)

11. And I was astounded

    to hear the little fellow (3)

      greet it with,(3, 2)

12. "No, no, no! I do not want an elephant

      inside a boa constrictor.(2)

13. A boa constrictor is

    a very dangerous creature,

      and an elephant is very cumbersome.(5)

14. Where I live,(5)

    everything is very small.

15. What I need is a sheep.(5)

      Draw me a sheep."

16. So then I made a drawing.

17. He looked

    at it carefully, then he said:(2)

18. "No. This sheep is already very sickly.

        Make me another."

19. So I made another drawing.

Step 2 구조 파악과 이해

My friend smiled gently and indulgently.

20. "You see yourself,"
　　　　he said, "that this is not a sheep.(5)

This is a ram.

　　　　It has horns."

21. So then I did my drawing over
　　　　　once more.

DAY 6

Step 1 원문 읽기

But it was rejected too, just like the others.

"This one is too old. I want a sheep that will live a long time."

By this time my patience was exhausted, because I was in a hurry to start taking my engine apart. So I tossed off this drawing.[1]

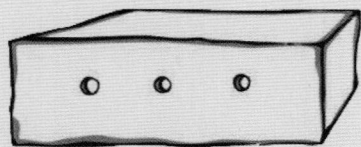

And I threw out an explanation with it.

"This is only his box. The sheep you asked for is inside."

I was very surprised to see a light break over the face of my young judge:[2]

"That is exactly the way I wanted it! Do you think that this sheep will have to have a great deal of grass?"
"Why?"
"Because where I live everything is very small..."
"There will surely be enough grass for him," I said. "It is a very small sheep that I have given you."

Step 1 원문 읽기

He bent his head over the drawing:

"Not so small that —Look! He has gone to sleep..."
And that is how I made the acquaintance of the little prince.³

It took me a long time to learn where he came from. The little prince, who asked me so many questions, never seemed to hear the ones I asked him.⁴ It was from words dropped by chance that, little by little, everything was revealed to me.⁵

The first time he saw my airplane, for instance(I shall not draw my airplane; that would be much too complicated for me), he asked me:

"What is that object?"

---

1. off 는 여기서 부사. 그림 그리고 툭 던지는 느낌.
2. light break? 이 상황에서 어린 왕자의 표정에 뭐가 있었을까요?
3. 이렇게 어린 왕자를 알게 되었어요.
4. prince seemed가 그 본형.
5. words dropped = 원래는 words that was dropped.

Step 2 구조 파악과 이해

01. But it was rejected too, just(4)
   　　　　　　　　like the others.(2)
02. "This one is too old. I want a sheep
   　　　　　　　that will live a long time."(5)
03. By this time(2)
   　　　my patience was exhausted,(4)
   　　　　　　because I was(5)
   　　　　　　　　in a hurry(2)
   　　　　　　　　　to start taking my engine apart.(3)
04. So I tossed off this drawing.
05. And I threw out an explanation
   　　　　　　　　with it.(2)
06. "This is only his box. The sheep
   　　　　　you asked for(5)
   　　　　　　　is inside."
07. I was very surprised(4)
   　　　to see a light break(3)
   　　　　　over the face (2)
   　　　　　　of my young judge:(2)
08. "That is exactly the way
   　　　I wanted it!(5)
09. Do you think
   　that this sheep will have(5)

Step 2 구조 파악과 이해

         to have a great deal(3)

           of grass?"(2)

"Why?"

10. "Because where I live(5)

    everything is very small..."

11. "There will surely be enough grass

    for him,"(2)

      I said.

"It is a very small sheep

    that I have given you."(5)

12. He bent his head

    over the drawing:(2)

13. "Not so small that — Look!

    He has gone to sleep..."

14. And that is how(5)

    I made the acquaintance

        of the little prince.(2)

15. It took me a long time

    to learn(3)

        where he came from.(5)

16. The little prince,

    who asked me so many questions,(5)

      never seemed

Step 2 구조 파악과 이해

to hear the ones(3)

I asked him.(5)

17. It was

    from words(2)

    dropped(4)

    by chance that, little by little,(2, 2)

    everything was revealed to me.(4, 2)

18. The first time he saw my airplane,

    for instance(2)

19. (I shall not draw my airplane;

    that would be much too complicated

    for me),(2)

20. he asked me:

21. "What is that object?"

DAY7

Step 3   1주차 지문을 한 번에 읽어봐요 : DAY 1

Once when I was six years old I saw a magnificent picture in a book. It was called *True Stories from Nature*, about the primeval forest. It was a picture of a boa constrictor in the act of swallowing an animal. Here is a copy of the drawing.

In the book it said: "Boa constrictors swallow their prey whole, without chewing it. After that they are not able to move, and they sleep through the six months that they need for digestion."

I pondered deeply, then, over the adventures of the jungle. And after some work with a colored pencil I succeeded in making my first drawing. My Drawing Number One. It looked like this:

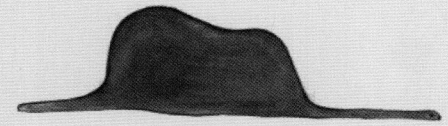

I showed my masterpiece to the grown-ups, and asked them whether the drawing frightened them. But they answered: "Frighten? Why should any one be frightened by a hat?"

 **Step 3** 1주차 지문을 한 번에 읽어봐요 : DAY 1

My drawing was not a picture of a hat. It was a picture of a boa constrictor digesting an elephant. But since the grown-ups were not able to understand it, I made another drawing: I drew the inside of the boa constrictor, so that the grown-ups could see it clearly.

They always need to have things explained. My Drawing Number Two looked like this:

Step 3 1주차 지문을 한 번에 읽어봐요 : DAY 2

The grown-ups' response, this time, was to advise me to lay aside my drawings. They said: "Don't draw boa constrictors, whether from the inside or the outside and devote yourself instead to geography, history, arithmetic, and grammar."

That is why, at the age of six, I gave up to be a magnificent career as a painter. I had been disheartened by the failure of my Drawing Number One and Two. Grown-ups never understand anything by themselves, and it is tiresome for children to be always and forever explaining things to them.

So then I chose another profession, and learned to pilot airplanes. I have flown a little over all parts of the world; and it is true that geography has been very useful to me. At a glance I can distinguish China from Arizona. If one gets lost in the night, such knowledge is valuable.

In the course of this life I have had a great many encounters with a many people. They have been concerned with matters of consequence.

I have lived a great deal among grown-ups. I have seen them intimately, close at hand. And that hasn't much improved my opinion of them.

 **Step 3** 1주차 지문을 한 번에 읽어봐요 : DAY 2

Whenever I met one of them who seemed to me at all clear-sighted, I tried the experiment of showing him my Drawing Number One, which I have always kept. I would try to find out, so, if this was a person of true understanding. But, whoever it was, he, or she, would always say:

"That is a hat."

Step 3 1주차 지문을 한 번에 읽어봐요 : DAY 3

Then I would never talk to that person about boa constrictors, or primeval forests, or stars. I would bring myself down to his level.

I would talk to him about bridge, and golf, and politics, and neckties.
And the grown-up would be greatly pleased to have met such a sensible man.

So I lived my life alone, without anyone that I could really talk to, until I had an accident with my plane in the Desert of Sahara, six years ago.

Something was broken in my engine. And as I had with me neither a mechanic nor any passengers, I set myself to attempt the difficult repairs all alone. It was a question of life or death for me: I had scarcely enough drinking water to last a week.

The first night, then, I went to sleep on the sand, a thousand miles from any human habitation. I was more isolated than a shipwrecked sailor on a raft in the middle of the ocean.

Thus you can imagine my amazement, at sunrise, when I was awakened by an odd little voice. It said:

Step 3   1주차 지문을 한 번에 읽어봐요 : DAY 3

"If you please – draw me a sheep!"
"What!"
"Draw me a sheep!"

I jumped to my feet, completely thunderstruck. I blinked my eyes hard. I looked carefully all around me.

And I saw a most extraordinary small person, who stood there examining me with great seriousness. Here you may see the best portrait that, later, I was able to make of him. But my drawing is certainly very much less charming than its model.

That, however, is not my fault. The grown-ups discouraged me in my painter's career when I was six years old, and I never learned to draw anything, except boas from the outside and boas from the inside.

Now I stared at this sudden apparition with my eyes fairly starting out of my head in astonishment. Remember, I had crashed in the desert a thousand miles from any inhabited region.

And yet my little man seemed neither to be straying uncertainly among the sands, nor to be fainting from fatigue or hunger or thirst or fear.

 **Step 3**   1주차 지문을 한 번에 읽어봐요 : DAY 4

Nothing about him gave any suggestion of a child lost in the middle of the desert, a thousand miles from any human habitation. When at last I was able to speak, I said to him:

"But – what are you doing here?"

And in answer he repeated, very slowly, as if he were speaking of a matter of great consequence:

"If you please – draw me a sheep..."

Step 3 1주차 지문을 한 번에 읽어봐요 : DAY 5

When a mystery is too overpowering, one dare not disobey. Absurd as it might seem to me, a thousand miles from any human habitation and in danger of death, I took out of my pocket a sheet of paper and my fountain-pen. Then I remembered how my studies had been concentrated on geography, history, and grammar, and I told the little chap that I did not know how to draw. He answered me:

"That doesn't matter. Draw me a sheep..."

But I had never drawn a sheep. So I drew for him one of the two pictures I had drawn so often. It was that of the boa constrictor from the outside. And I was astounded to hear the little fellow greet it with,

"No, no, no! I do not want an elephant inside a boa constrictor. A boa constrictor is a very dangerous creature, and an elephant is very cumbersome. Where I live, everything is very small. What I need is a sheep. Draw me a sheep."

So then I made a drawing.

He looked at it carefully, then he said:

"No. This sheep is already very sickly. Make me another."

So I made another drawing.

My friend smiled gently and indulgently.

"You see yourself," he said, "that this is not a sheep. This is a ram. It has horns."

So then I did my drawing over once more.

But it was rejected too, just like the others.

"This one is too old. I want a sheep that will live a long time."

By this time my patience was exhausted, because I was in a hurry to start taking my engine apart. So I tossed off this drawing.

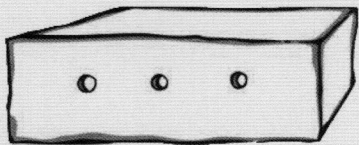

And I threw out an explanation with it.

"This is only his box. The sheep you asked for is inside."

I was very surprised to see a light break over the face of my young judge:

"That is exactly the way I wanted it! Do you think that this sheep will have to have a great deal of grass?"
"Why?"
"Because where I live everything is very small..."
"There will surely be enough grass for him," I said. "It is a very small sheep that I have given you."

 **1주차 지문을 한 번에 읽어봐요 : DAY 6**

He bent his head over the drawing:

"Not so small that —Look! He has gone to sleep..."
And that is how I made the acquaintance of the little prince.

It took me a long time to learn where he came from. The little prince, who asked me so many questions, never seemed to hear the ones I asked him. It was from words dropped by chance that, little by little, everything was revealed to me.

The first time he saw my airplane, for instance (I shall not draw my airplane: that would be much too complicated for me), he asked me:

"What is that object?"

WEEK 2

계속 강조하지만, 단어 뜻과 문장 뜻을 '한국어로' 일일이 알려하지 마세요. 우리가 해야 할 1순위는 '구조 파악'입니다. 한국어로 된 어려운 철학책을 읽고 이해 못 한다고 기본적인 한국어에 문제가 있는 건 아닌 것과 같아요. 구조 파악이 되고 나면 전체적 이야기의 흐름도 파악되면 좋아요. 머릿속에 이미지가 어느 정도 남으면 됩니다.

Step 1 원문 읽기

"That is not an object. It flies. It is an airplane. It is my airplane."

And I was proud to have him learn that I could fly.[1]

He cried out, then:

"What! You dropped down from the sky?"
"Yes," I answered, modestly.
"Oh! That is funny!"

And the little prince broke into a lovely peal of laughter, which irritated me very much.[2] I like my misfortunes to be taken seriously.[3] Then he added:

"So you, too, come from the sky! Which is your planet?"

At that moment I caught a gleam of light in the impenetrable mystery of his presence;[4] and I demanded, abruptly:

"Do you come from another planet?"

But he did not reply. He tossed his head gently, without taking his eyes from my plane:

Step 1 원문 읽기

"It is true that on that you can't have come from very far away..."⁵

And he sank into a reverie, which lasted a long time. Then, taking my sheep out of his pocket, he buried himself in the contemplation of his treasure.

You can imagine how my curiosity was aroused by this half-confidence about the "other planets." I made a great effort, therefore, to find out more on this subject.

"My little man, where do you come from? What is this 'where I live,' of which you speak? Where do you want to take your sheep?"

After a reflective silence he answered:

"The thing that is so good about the box you have given me is that at night he can use it as his house."⁶

---

1. I'm proud to have you (to) learn English.
2. Prince B into P of L.
3. 내 불운이 to be taken(받아들여지길) 진지하게 : 비행기 사고 났다는데 어린 왕자가 웃어서 기분 상한 것.
4. 연습하기 좋네요! gleam이나 impenetrable이란 단어 뜻 몰라도 돼요. at the moment, I C a G of L in M of P.
5. It is true that on that(plane) you can't...
6. 기본은 thing is that으로 끝. 0 해 안 되면 말문 트기 편 '관계사'를 더 연습하세요. 관계사가 3개 들어가 있어요.

Step 2   구조 파악과 이해

01. "That is not an object. It flies.

                       It is an airplane. It is my airplane."

02. And I was proud

       to have him(3)

          learn that I could fly.(3, 5)

03. He cried out, then:

             "What! You dropped down

                   from the sky?"(2)

04. "Yes," I answered, modestly.

               "Oh! That is funny!"

05. And the little prince broke

           into a lovely peal(2)

             of laughter,(2)

                 which irritated me very much.(5)

06. I like my misfortunes

           to be taken seriously.(3, 4)

              Then he added:

07. "So you, too, come from the sky!

              Which is your planet?"

08. At that moment(2)

      I caught a gleam

         of light(2)

           in the impenetrable mystery(2)

Step 2 구조 파악과 이해

　　　　　　　　　　　of his presence;(2)
09. and I demanded, abruptly:
　　　"Do you come
　　　　　from another planet?"(2)
10. But he did not reply.
　　He tossed his head gently,
　　　　without taking his eyes(2, 4)
　　　　　　from my plane:(2)
11. "It is true that(5)
　　　　on that(2)
　　　　　　you can't have come
　　　　　　　　from very far away…"(2)
12. And he sank
　　　into a reverie,(2)
　　　　which lasted a long time.(2)
13. Then, taking my sheep out(4)
　　　of his pocket,(2)
　　　　he buried himself
　　　　　in the contemplation(2)
　　　　　　of his treasure.(2)
14. You can imagine
　　　how my curiosity was aroused(4)
　　　　by this half-confidence(2)

Step 2 구조 파악과 이해

　　　　　　　　　　　　　　about the "other planets."(2)
15. I made a great effort, therefore,
　　　　　　　　　　to find out more(3)
　　　　　　　　　　　on this subject.(2)
16. "My little man,
　　　　　　　　where do you come from?
　What is this
　　　　　'where I live,'(5)
　　　　　　　of which you speak?(2)
17. Where do you want
　　　　　　to take your sheep?"(3)
　　　　　　　　　After a reflective silence(2)
　　　　　　　　　　　　　he answered:
18. "The thing
　　　　that is so good(5)
　　　　　　about the box(2)
　　　　　　　(that) you have given me is(5)
　　　　　　　　　that at night(5, 2)
　　　　　　　　　　　he can use it
　　　　　　　　　　　　　as his house."(2)

DAY 9

Step 1 원문 읽기

"That is so.[1] And if you are good I will give you a string, too, so that you can tie him during the day, and a post to tie him to."

But the little prince seemed shocked by this offer:[2]

"Tie him! What a queer idea!"
"But if you don't tie him," I said, "he will wander off somewhere, and get lost."

My friend broke into another peal of laughter:

"But where do you think he would go?"
"Anywhere. Straight ahead of him."

Then the little prince said, earnestly:

"That doesn't matter. Where I live, everything is so small!"

And, with perhaps a hint of sadness, he added:

"Straight ahead of him, nobody can go very far…"

I had thus learned a second fact of great importance: this was that the planet the little prince came from was scarcely any larger than

Step 1 원문 읽기

a house![3]

But that did not really surprise me much. I knew very well that in addition to the great planets — such as the Earth, Jupiter, Mars, Venus — to which we have given names, there are also hundreds of others, some of which are so small that one has a hard time seeing them through the telescope.

When an astronomer discovers one of these he does not give it a name, but only a number. He might call it, for example, "Asteroid 325."

---
1. That is so : 여기선 '그렇지' 정도.
2. The prince seemed S—ed by O.
3. this was that P was L = this was that. 이 책 was good. 'the planet (that) the prince came...'

Step 2 구조 파악과 이해

01. "That is so.
    And if you are good(5)
    I will give you a string, too.
02. So that you can tie him
    during the day, and a post(2)
    to tie him to."(3, 2)
03. But the little prince seemed
    shocked(4)
    by this offer:(2)
04. "Tie him! What a queer idea!"
05. "But if you don't tie him," I said,
    "he will wander
    off somewhere, and get lost."(2, 4)
06. My friend broke
    into another peal(2)
    of laughter:(2)
07. "But where do you think
    he would go?"(5)
08. "Anywhere. Straight ahead
    of him."(2)
    Then the little prince said, earnestly:
09. "That doesn't matter.
    Where I live, everything is so small!"(5)

Step 2 구조 파악과 이해

10. And, with perhaps a hint(2)
        of sadness, he added:(2)

11. "Straight ahead
        of him, nobody can go very far..."(2)

12. I had thus learned a second fact
        of great importance:(2)

13. this was
        that the planet the little prince came(5)
            from was scarcely any larger(2)
                than a house!(2)

14. But that did not really surprise me much.

15. I knew very well
        that in addition(5, 2)
            to the great planets –(2)
              such as the Earth,(2)
                    Jupiter, Mars, Venus –

16. to which(2, 5)
    we have given names,
        there are also hundreds
            of others,(2)

17. some of which are so small(2)
    that one has a hard time(5)
        seeing them(4)

Step 2 구조 파악과 이해

　　　　　　　　　　　　through the telescope.(2)
18. When an astronomer discovers one(5)
　　　　　　　　　　of these(2)
　　　　　　　　　　　　he does not give it a name,
　　　　　　　　　　　　　　　　but only a number.(5)
19. He might call it,
　　　　　　for example, "Asteroid 325."

DAY10

Step 1 원문 읽기

I have reason to believe that the planet from which the little prince came is the asteroid known as B-612.¹

This asteroid has only once been seen through the telescope. That was by a Turkish astronomer, in 1909.

On making his discovery, he had presented it to the International Astronomical Congress, in a great demonstration. But he was in Turkish costume, and so nobody would believe what he said.

Grown-ups are like that...

Fortunately, however, for the reputation of Asteroid B-612, a Turkish dictator made a law. The law that his subjects, under pain of death, should change to European costume.² So in 1920 the astronomer gave his demonstration all over again, dressed with

Step 1 원문 읽기

impressive style and elegance. And this time everybody accepted his report.

If I have told you these details about the asteroid, and made a note of its number for you, it is on account of the grown-ups and their ways.³ When you tell them that you have made a new friend, they never ask you any questions about essential matters.

They never say to you, "What does his voice sound like? What games does he love best? Does he collect butterflies?" Instead, they demand: "How old is he? How many brothers has he? How much does he weigh? How much money does his father make?" Only from these figures do they think they have learned anything about him.⁴

---

1. believe that the planet is the A.
2. The L that S should C to E C. 동사가 없으므로 문장 아니에요.
3. it is on account ~ 부터가 기본문.
4. do they think는 질문이 아니라 강조하느라 do를 넣은 것.

Step 2 구조 파악과 이해

01. I have reason
　　　to believe(3)
　　　　　that the planet(5)
　　　　　　　from which the little prince came(2, 5)
　　　　　　　　　is the asteroid
　　　　　　　　　　　known as B-612.(4)

02. This asteroid has only once been seen(4)
　　　　　　　through the telescope.(2)

03. That was
　　　by a Turkish astronomer, in 1909.(2)

04. On making his discovery,(2, 4)
　　　he had presented it
　　　　　to the International Astronomical Congress,(2)
　　　　　　　in a great demonstration.(2)

05. But he was
　　　in Turkish costume,(2)
　　　　　and so nobody would believe
　　　　　　　what he said.(5)

06. Grown-ups are
　　　like that...(2)

07. Fortunately, however,
　　　for the reputation(2)
　　　　　of Asteroid B-612,(2)

Step 2 구조 파악과 이해

　　　　　　　　　　　　　a Turkish dictator made a law.
08. The law that his subjects, (5)
　　　under pain(2)
　　　　　of death,(2)
　　　　　　　should change
　　　　　　　　　to European costume.
09. So in 1920(2)
　　　the astronomer gave his demonstration
　　　　　all over again,
　　　　　　　dressed(4)
　　　　　　　　　with impressive style and elegance.(2)
10. And this time everybody accepted
　　　　　　　　　his report.
11. If I have told you these details(5)
　　　　　about the asteroid,(2)
　　　　　　　and made a note
　　　　　　　　　of its number(2)
　　　　　　　　　　　for you,(2)
12. it is
　　　on account(2)
　　　　　of the grown-ups and their ways.(2)
13. When you tell them(5)
　　　that you have made a new friend,(5)

Step 2 구조 파악과 이해

        they never ask you any questions(5)

            about essential matters.(2)

14. They never say to you,

    "What does his voice sound like?

        What games does he love best?

15. Does he collect butterflies?"

  Instead, they demand: "How old is he?

      How many brothers has he?

16. How much does he weigh?

      How much money does his father make?"

17. Only from(2)

    these figures

      do they think

        they have learned anything(5)

           about him.(2)

DAY11

Step 1 원문 읽기

If you were to say to the grown-ups: "I saw a beautiful house made of rosy brick,[1] with geraniums in the windows and doves on the roof," they would not be able[2] to get any idea of that house at all.

You would have to say to them: "I saw a house that cost $ 20,000." Then they would exclaim: "Oh, what a pretty house that is!"

Just so, you might say to them: "The proof that the little prince existed is that he was charming,[3] that he laughed, and that he was looking for a sheep. If anybody wants a sheep, that is a proof that he exists."

And what good would it do to tell them that? They would shrug[4] their shoulders, and treat you like a child. But if you said to them: "The planet he came from is Asteroid B-612," then they would be convinced, and leave you in peace from their questions.

They are like that. One must not hold it against them. Children should always show great forbearance toward grown-up people.

But certainly, for us who understand life, figures are a matter of indifference. I should have liked to begin this story in the fashion of the fairy-tales.

Step 1 원문 읽기

I should have like to say: "Once upon a time there was a little prince who lived on a planet that was scarcely any bigger than himself, and who had need of a sheep…"

To those who understand life, that would have given a much greater air of truth to my story.

For I do not want any one to read my book carelessly. I have suffered too much grief in setting down these memories.

---
1. I saw a house made of brick.
2. able : if you are able to do something, you have skills for you to do it.
3. proof is that이 (1).
4. shrug : if you shrug, you raise your shoulders.

Step 2 구조 파악과 이해

01. If you were
      to say to the grown-ups:(3, 2)

02. "I saw a beautiful house
      made of rosy brick,(4, 2)
            with geraniums(2)
                  in the windows and doves(2, 5)
                        on the roof,"(2)

03. they would not be able
      to get any idea(3)
            of that house at all.(2)

04. You would have
      to say to them: "I saw a house(3, 2)
            that cost $ 20,000."(5)

05. Then they would exclaim:
      "Oh, what a pretty house that is!"

06. Just so, you might say to them: (2)
      "The proof
            that the little prince existed is(5)
                  that he was charming,(5)

07. that he laughed,(5)
      and that he was looking(5)
            for a sheep.(2)

08. If anybody wants a sheep,(5)

Step 2 구조 파악과 이해

　　　　　that is a proof(5)
　　　　　　　that he exists."(5)
09. And what good would it do
　　　　　　to tell them that?(3)
10. They would shrug their shoulders,
　　　　　　　and treat you(5)
　　　　　　　　like a child.(2)
11. But if you said to them:(2)
　　　　　"The planet
　　　　　　he came from(5, 2)
　　　　　　　is Asteroid B-612,"
12. then they would be convinced,
　　　　　and leave you
　　　　　　　in peace from their questions.(2, 2)
13. They are like that. One must not hold it(2)
　　　　　　against them.(2)
14. Children should always show
　　　　　great forbearance
　　　　　　toward grown-up people.(2)
15. But certainly, for us(2)
　　　who understand life,(5)
　　　　figures are a matter
　　　　　　of indifference.(2)

Step 2 구조 파악과 이해

16. I should have liked
    to begin this story(3)
        in the fashion(2)
            of the fairy-tales.(2)
                I should have like to say:(3)

17. "Once upon a time
    there was a little prince
        who lived on a planet(5, 2)

18. that was scarcely any bigger
    than himself,(2)
        and who had need(5)
            of a sheep..."(2)

19. To those who understand life,(2, 5)
    that would have given
        a much greater air
            of truth(2)
                to my story.(2)

20. For I do not want any one(5)
    to read my book carelessly.(3)

21. I have suffered too much grief
    in setting down these memories.(2, 4)

DAY12

Step 1 원문 읽기

Six years have already passed since my friend went away from me, with his sheep. If I try to describe him here, it is to make sure that I shall not forget him.[1]

To forget a friend is sad. Not every one has had a friend. If I forget him, I am like the grown-ups who are no longer interested in anything but figures...

It is for that purpose, again, that I have bought a box of paints and some pencils. It is hard to take up drawing again at my age, when I have never made any pictures except those of the boa constrictor, since I was six.

I shall certainly try to make my portraits as true to life as possible.[2] But I am not at all sure of success. One drawing goes along all right, and another has no resemblance to its subject.

I make some errors, too, in the little prince's height: in one place he is too tall and in another too short. And I feel some doubts about the color of his costume. So I fumble along as best I can, now good, now bad, and I hope generally fair-to-middling.[3]

In certain more important details I shall make mistakes, also. But that is something that will not be my fault. My friend never

Step 1 원문 읽기

explained anything to me. He thought, perhaps, that I was like himself.

But I, alas, do not know how to see sheep through the walls of boxes. Perhaps I am a little like the grown-ups. I have had to grow old.

전 이 부분 보면서 몇 번이나 눈물이 날 뻔… 내용이 정말 아름답네요…
1. It is가 (1)이에요. 조금 더 붙이면 It is to make sure : 확실히 하려고(그를 절대 잊지 않으려고).
2. as true to life… 부분이 구조를 따지자면 좀 복잡하고 애매한데, '최대한 사실에 가깝게' 정도의 느낌만 가지고 일단 넘어가죠! ^^
3. fumble, fair-to-middling의 '한국어 뜻'을 알려 하지 마세요. (저도 모릅니다. 물론 사전 검색하면 나오겠죠.) 문장 구조 이해하는데 문제없고, 대략 앞뒤 문장 사이에서 흐름 파악하는 정도로 가는 게 좋아요. 문법 공부가 아니라 '독서'를 하고 있는 거예요, 우린.

Step 2 구조 파악과 이해

01. Six years have **already** passed
   since my friend went away(5)
      from me,(2)
       with his sheep.(2)

02. If I try(5)
   to describe him here,(3)
     it is
      to make sure(3)
       that I shall not forget him.(5)

03. To forget a friend is sad.
   Not every one has had a friend.

04. If I forget him,(5)
   I am like the grown-ups
     who are no longer interested(5)
      in anything but figures...(2)

05. It is
   for that purpose, again,(2)
     that I have bought a box(5)
      of paints and some pencils.(2)

06. It is hard
   to take up drawing again(3)
     at my age,(2)

07. when I have never made any pictures(5)

Step 2 구조 파악과 이해

　　　except those of the boa constrictor.(2, 2)
　　　　　since I was six.(5)
08. I shall certainly try
　　　to make my portraits(3)
　　　　　as true to life as possible.(2, 2, 2)
09. But I am not
　　　at all sure(2)
　　　　　of success.(2)
10. One drawing goes along all right,
　　　and another has no resemblance
　　　　　to its subject.(2)
11. I make some errors, too,
　　　in the little prince's height:(2)
12. in one place(2)
　　　he is too tall
　　　　　and in another too short.(2)
13. And I feel some doubts
　　　about the color(2)
　　　　　of his costume.(2)
14. So I fumble along
　　　as best I can, now good, now bad,(5)
　　　　　and I hope generally fair-to-middling.
15. In certain more important details(2)

Step 2 구조 파악과 이해

              I shall make mistakes, also.

16. But that is something

        that will not be my fault.(5)

17. My friend never explained anything

              to me.(2)

18. He thought, perhaps,

      that I was(5)

      like himself.(2)

19. But I, alas, do not know

    how to see sheep(5, 3)

      through the walls(2)

        of boxes.(2)

20. Perhaps I am a little

      like the grown-ups.(2)

        I have had

          to grow old.(3)

DAY 13

Step 1 원문 읽기

As each day passed I would learn, in our talk, something about the little prince's things. The information would come very slowly, as it might chance to fall from his thoughts. It was in this way that I heard, on the third day, about the catastrophe of the baobabs.

This time, once more, I had the sheep to thank for it. For the little prince asked me abruptly – as if seized by a grave doubt – "It is true, isn't it, that sheep eat little bushes?"

"Yes, that is true."
"Ah! I am glad!"

I did not understand why it was so important that sheep should eat little bushes. But the little prince added:

"Then it follows that they also eat baobabs?"[1]

I pointed out to the little prince that baobabs were not little bushes, but, trees as big as castles; and that even if he took a whole herd of elephants away with him, the herd would not eat up one single baobab.

The idea of the herd of elephants made the little prince laugh.[2]

Step 1 원문 읽기

"We would have to put them one on top of the other," he said.

But he made a wise comment:

"Before they grow so big, the baobabs start out by being little."
"That is strictly correct," I said. "But why do you want the sheep to eat the little baobabs?"

He answered me at once, "Oh, come, come!", as if he were speaking of something that was self-evident. And I was obliged to make a great mental effort to solve this problem, without any assistance.

---

1. then it follows : 여기선 '그러면' 정도가 될 듯.
2. the idea made the prince (to) laugh.

Step 2 구조 파악과 이해

01. As each day passed(5)
  I would learn,
    in our talk,(2)
      something
        about the little prince's things.(2)

02. The information would come very slowly,
    as it might chance(5)
      to fall(3)
        from his thoughts.(2)

03. It was
  in this way(2)
    that I heard,(5)
      on the third day,(2)
        about the catastrophe(2)
          of the baobabs.(2)

04. This time, once more, I had the sheep
      to thank for it.(3, 2)

05. For the little prince asked me abruptly(5)
    —as if seized(5, 4)
      by a grave doubt —(2)

06. "It is true, isn't it,
  that sheep eat little bushes?"

07. "Yes, that is true."

Step 2 구조 파악과 이해

"Ah! I am glad!"
08. I did not understand
    why it was so important(5)
        that sheep should eat little bushes.(5)
09. But the little prince added:
    "Then it follows
        that they also eat baobabs?"(5)
10. I pointed out
    to the little prince(2)
    that baobabs were not little bushes,(5)
        but, trees as big as castles;(2, 2)
11. and that even if he took a whole herd(5)
    of elephants away(2)
        with him,(2)
12. the herd would not eat up
    one single baobab.
13. The idea
    of the herd(2)
    of elephants(2)
        made the little prince laugh.(3)
14. "We would have
    to put them one(3)
        on top(2)

Step 2 구조 파악과 이해

of the other," he said.(2)

15. But he made a wise comment:

    "Before they grow so big,

        the baobabs start out

            by being little."(2)

16. "That is strictly correct," I said.

    "But why do you want the sheep

        to eat the little baobabs?"(3)

17. He answered me at once,

    "Oh, come, come!",

18. as if he were speaking(5)

    of something(2)

        that was self-evident.(5)

19. And I was obliged

    to make a great mental effort(3)

    to solve this problem.(3)

    without any assistance.(2)

DAY14

Step 3   2주차 지문을 한 번에 읽어봐요 : DAY 8

"That is not an object. It flies. It is an airplane. It is my airplane."

And I was proud to have him learn that I could fly.

He cried out, then:

"What! You dropped down from the sky?"
"Yes," I answered, modestly.
"Oh! That is funny!"

And the little prince broke into a lovely peal of laughter, which irritated me very much. I like my misfortunes to be taken seriously. Then he added:

"So you, too, come from the sky! Which is your planet?"

At that moment I caught a gleam of light in the impenetrable mystery of his presence; and I demanded, abruptly:

"Do you come from another planet?"

But he did not reply. He tossed his head gently, without taking his eyes from my plane:

 **2주차 지문을 한 번에 읽어봐요 : DAY 8**

"It is true that on that you can't have come from very far away..."

And he sank into a reverie, which lasted a long time. Then, taking my sheep out of his pocket, he buried himself in the contemplation of his treasure.

You can imagine how my curiosity was aroused by this half-confidence about the "other planets." I made a great effort, therefore, to find out more on this subject.

"My little man, where do you come from? What is this 'where I live,' of which you speak? Where do you want to take your sheep?"

After a reflective silence he answered:

"The thing that is so good about the box you have given me is that at night he can use it as his house."

Step 3 2주차 지문을 한 번에 읽어봐요 : DAY 9

"That is so. And if you are good I will give you a string, too, so that you can tie him during the day, and a post to tie him to."

But the little prince seemed shocked by this offer:

"Tie him! What a queer idea!"
"But if you don't tie him," I said, "he will wander off somewhere, and get lost."

My friend broke into another peal of laughter:

"But where do you think he would go?"
"Anywhere. Straight ahead of him."

Then the little prince said, earnestly:

"That doesn't matter. Where I live, everything is so small!"

And, with perhaps a hint of sadness, he added:

"Straight ahead of him, nobody can go very far..."

I had thus learned a second fact of great importance: this was that the planet the little prince came from was scarcely any larger than

Step 3   2주차 지문을 한 번에 읽어봐요 : DAY 9

a house!

But that did not really surprise me much. I knew very well that in addition to the great planets – such as the Earth, Jupiter, Mars, Venus – to which we have given names, there are also hundreds of others, some of which are so small that one has a hard time seeing them through the telescope.

When an astronomer discovers one of these he does not give it a name, but only a number. He might call it, for example, "Asteroid 325."

Step 3 2주차 지문을 한 번에 읽어봐요 : DAY 10

I have reason to believe that the planet from which the little prince came is the asteroid known as B-612.

This asteroid has only once been seen through the telescope. That was by a Turkish astronomer, in 1909.

On making his discovery, he had presented it to the International Astronomical Congress, in a great demonstration. But he was in Turkish costume, and so nobody would believe what he said.

Grown-ups are like that...

Fortunately, however, for the reputation of Asteroid B-612, a Turkish dictator made a law. The law that his subjects, under pain of death, should change to European costume. So in 1920 the astronomer gave his demonstration all over again, dressed with impressive style and elegance. And this time everybody accepted his report.

If I have told you these details about the asteroid, and made a note of its number for you, it is on account of the grown-ups and their ways. When you tell them that you have made a new friend, they never ask you any questions about essential matters.

They never say to you, "What does his voice sound like? What games does he love best? Does he collect butterflies?" Instead, they demand: "How old is he? How many brothers has he? How much does he weigh? How much money does his father make?" Only from these figures do they think they have learned anything about him.

Step 3　2주차 지문을 한 번에 읽어봐요 : DAY 11

If you were to say to the grown-ups: "I saw a beautiful house made of rosy brick, with geraniums in the windows and doves on the roof," they would not be able to get any idea of that house at all.

You would have to say to them: "I saw a house that cost $ 20,000." Then they would exclaim: "Oh, what a pretty house that is!"

Just so, you might say to them: "The proof that the little prince existed is that he was charming, that he laughed, and that he was looking for a sheep. If anybody wants a sheep, that is a proof that he exists."

And what good would it do to tell them that? They would shrug their shoulders, and treat you like a child. But if you said to them: "The planet he came from is Asteroid B-612," then they would be convinced, and leave you in peace from their questions.

They are like that. One must not hold it against them. Children should always show great forbearance toward grown-up people.

But certainly, for us who understand life, figures are a matter of indifference. I should have liked to begin this story in the fashion of the fairy-tales.

 **Step 3**   2주차 지문을 한 번에 읽어봐요 : DAY 11

I should have like to say: "Once upon a time there was a little prince who lived on a planet that was scarcely any bigger than himself, and who had need of a sheep…"

To those who understand life, that would have given a much greater air of truth to my story.

For I do not want any one to read my book carelessly. I have suffered too much grief in setting down these memories.

Step 3 2주차 지문을 한 번에 읽어봐요 : DAY 12

Six years have already passed since my friend went away from me, with his sheep. If I try to describe him here, it is to make sure that I shall not forget him.

To forget a friend is sad. Not every one has had a friend. If I forget him, I am like the grown-ups who are no longer interested in anything but figures...

It is for that purpose, again, that I have bought a box of paints and some pencils. It is hard to take up drawing again at my age, when I have never made any pictures except those of the boa constrictor, since I was six.

I shall certainly try to make my portraits as true to life as possible. But I am not at all sure of success. One drawing goes along all right, and another has no resemblance to its subject.

I make some errors, too, in the little prince's height: in one place he is too tall and in another too short. And I feel some doubts about the color of his costume. So I fumble along as best I can, now good, now bad, and I hope generally fair-to-middling.

In certain more important details I shall make mistakes, also. But that is something that will not be my fault. My friend never

 **Step 3** 2주차 지문을 한 번에 읽어봐요 : DAY 12

explained anything to me. He thought, perhaps, that I was like himself.

But I, alas, do not know how to see sheep through the walls of boxes. Perhaps I am a little like the grown-ups. I have had to grow old.

Step 3　2주차 지문을 한 번에 읽어봐요 : DAY 13

As each day passed I would learn, in our talk, something about the little prince's things. The information would come very slowly, as it might chance to fall from his thoughts. It was in this way that I heard, on the third day, about the catastrophe of the baobabs.

This time, once more, I had the sheep to thank for it. For the little prince asked me abruptly — as if seized by a grave doubt — "It is true, isn't it, that sheep eat little bushes?"

"Yes, that is true."
"Ah! I am glad!"

I did not understand why it was so important that sheep should eat little bushes. But the little prince added:

"Then it follows that they also eat baobabs?"

I pointed out to the little prince that baobabs were not little bushes, but, trees as big as castles; and that even if he took a whole herd of elephants away with him, the herd would not eat up one single baobab.

The idea of the herd of elephants made the little prince laugh.

Step 3   2주차 지문을 한 번에 읽어봐요 : DAY 13

"We would have to put them one on top of the other," he said.

But he made a wise comment:

"Before they grow so big, the baobabs start out by being little."
"That is strictly correct," I said. "But why do you want the sheep to eat the little bacbabs?"

He answered me at once, "Oh, come, come!", as if he were speaking of something that was self-evident. And I was obliged to make a great mental effort to solve this problem, without any assistance.

WEEK 3

'단어 뜻도 안 알려주고, 일일이 찾아보지 말라고 하고 뭐 이런 영어책이 있어?' 할 수 있어요. 그런데 이게 맞는 방법입니다. 기존 방법이 맞았으면 한국인들 영어가 이 모양이 되진 않았을 거예요. 기존 방법은 계속해와서 익숙하지만 안 되는 방법이에요. 바꿔야 합니다. '시치미' '어처구니' '거덜 난다' 등 우리도 뜻을 정확히 모르고 문맥상으로 이해하는 한국어 많아요.

DAY15

Step 1 원문 읽기

There were good plants and bad plants on the planet where the little prince lived — as on all planets. In consequence, there were good seeds from good plants, and bad seeds from bad plants.

But seeds are invisible. They sleep deep in the heart of the earth's darkness. Until some one among them is seized with the desire to awaken.[1] Then this little seed will stretch itself timidly at first. They push a charming little sprig inoffensively upward toward the sun.[2]

If it is only a sprig of radish or rose-bush, one would let it grow wherever it might wish.[3] But when it is a bad plant, one must destroy it as soon as possible, the very first instant that one recognizes it.

Now there were some terrible seeds on the planet that was the home of the little prince; and these were the seeds of the baobab. The soil of that planet was infested with them.

A baobab is something you will never, never be able to get rid of if you attend to it too late. It spreads over the entire planet. It bores clear through it with its roots.[4] And if the planet is too small, and the baobabs are too many, they split it in pieces...

"It is a question of discipline," the little prince said to me later on.

Step 1 원문 읽기

"When you've finished your own toilet in the morning, then it is time for your planet for the toilet.

You must see to it that you pull up regularly all the baobabs, at the very first moment when they can be distinguished from the rosebushes.[5] Because they resemble so closely in their earliest youth. It is very tedious work," the little prince added, "but very easy."

---

1. one is seized with D.
2. They P a sprig toward S.
3. one would let it (to) grow.
4. it bores + (2) + (2) 구조. 무슨 뜻인지 몰라도 일단 구조 파악이 우선! bore가 여기선 지루한 거 말고 '보링머신(구멍 뚫는 기계)'에서의 '뚫다'로 쓰였어요.
5. at the very first moment ~ 은 문장이 아니고 그냥 '제일 첫 순간'이라는 설명.

Step 2 구조 파악과 이해

01. There were good plants and bad plants
      on the planet(2)
          where the little prince lived(5)
              —as on all planets.(2)

02. In consequence,(2)
    there were good seeds
        from good plants, and bad seeds(2, 5)
              from bad plants.(2)

03. But seeds are invisible.
  They sleep deep
      in the heart of the earth's darkness.(2, 2)

04. Until some one(5)
      among them is seized(2, 4)
          with the desire to awaken.(2, 3)

05. Then this little seed will stretch itself
                timidly at first.(2)

06. They push a charming little sprig
    inoffensively upward
        toward the sun.(2)

07. If it is only a sprig(5)
    of radish or rose-bush,(2)
      one would let it grow(3)
          wherever it might wish.(5)

Step 2 구조 파악과 이해

08. But when it is a bad plant,
    one must destroy it
        as soon as possible,(2)
            the very first instant
                that one recognizes it.(5)

09. Now there were some terrible seeds
    on the planet that was the home(2, 5)
        of the little prince;(2)

10. and these were the seeds
    of the baobab.(2)

The soil
    of that planet was infested(2, 4)
        with them.(2)

11. A baobab is something
    you will never, never be able
        to get rid of(3)
            if you attend to it too late.(5, 2)

12. It spreads
    over the entire planet.(2)

It bores clear
    through it(2)
        with its roots.(2)

13. And if the planet is too small,(5)

Step 2 구조 파악과 이해

   and the baobabs are too many,
     they split it
       in pieces...(2)

14. "It is a question
   of discipline,"(2)
     the little prince said
       to me later on.(2)

15. "When you've finished your own toilet(5)
   in the morning,(2)
     then it is time(5)
       for your planet(2)
        for the toilet.(2)

16. You must see
   to it(2)
     that you pull up regularly
       all the baobabs,

17. at the very first moment(2)
   when they can be distinguished(5)
     from the rosebushes.(2)

18. Because they resemble so closely
   in their earliest youth.(2)

19. It is very tedious work,"
   the little prince added, "but very easy."

DAY 16

Step 1 원문 읽기

And one day he said to me: "You ought to make a beautiful drawing, so that the children where you live can see exactly how all this is.[1] That would be very useful to them if they were to travel some day. Sometimes," he added, "there is no harm in putting off a piece of work until another day. But when it is a matter of baobabs, that always means a catastrophe.[2] I knew a planet that was inhabited by a lazy man. He neglected three little bushes..."

So, as the little prince described it to me, I have made a drawing of that planet. I do not like to take the tone of a moralist.

But the danger of the baobabs is so little understood, and such considerable risks would be run by anyone who might get lost on an asteroid,[3] that for once I am breaking through my reserve. "Children," I say, "watch out for the baobabs!"

My friends, like myself, have been skirting this danger for a long time, without ever knowing it;[4] and so it is for them that I have worked so hard over this drawing. The lesson which I pass on by this means is worth all the trouble it has cost me.[5]

Perhaps you will ask me, "Why are there no other drawing in this book as impressive as this drawing of the baobabs?"

Step 1 원문 읽기

The reply is simple. I have tried. But with the others I have not been successful. When I made the drawing of the baobabs I was carried beyond myself by the urgent necessity.[6]

---

1. children can see가 기본형!
2. that means가 (1).
3. risks would be run by A who might get on A 흔태. '그런 위험은 누구에게나 / 길 잃는 / 행성에서' 정도.
4. friend have been skirting이 (1). skirt가 동사로 쓰였네요? 이게 무슨 뜻일까요? 계속 강조하지만 구조 파악이 1순위. 파악됐으면 문맥상으로 뜻 추측이 되기도 하니까요. 우리말 책 볼 때와 같다고 했습니다.
5. lesson is worth가 (1). '수고해서 그린 이 그림만큼 이 교훈(바오밥을 조심해)은 가치 있다' 정도인데요. 관계사도 두 거 있고, 너무 복잡하면 일단 넘어가고 나중에 다시 보는 것도 방법!
6. I was carried가 (1). 위험을 알리고자 하는 마음에 carried(움직여졌다).

Step 2 구조 파악과 이해

01. And one day he said
    to me:(2)
        "You ought
            to make a beautiful drawing,(3)

02. so that the children(5)
    where you live can see exactly(5)
        how all this is.(5)

03. That would be very useful
    to them(2)
        if they were(5)
            to travel some day.(3)

04. Sometimes," he added,
    "there is no harm
        in putting(2)
            off a piece(2)
        of work(2)
        until another day.(2)

05. But when it is a matter(5)
    of baobabs,(2)
        that always means a catastrophe.

06. I knew a planet
    that was inhabited(5)
    by a lazy man.(2)

Step 2 구조 파악과 이해

He neglected three little bushes…"
07. So, as the little prince described it(5)
　　to me,(2)
　　　　I have made a drawing
　　　　　　of that planet.(2)
08. I do not like
　　to take the tone(3)
　　　　of a moralist.(2)
But the danger
　　of the baobabs(2)
　　　　is so little understood,(4)
09. and such considerable risks would be run
　　by anyone(2)
　　　　who might get lost(5, 4)
　　　　　　on an asteroid,(2)
10. that for once I am breaking
　　through my reserve.(2)
"Children," I say,
　　"watch out for the baobabs!"
11. My friends, like myself,
　　have been skirting this danger(4)
　　　　for a long time,(2)
　　　　　　without ever knowing it;(2, 4)

Step 2 구조 파악과 이해

12. and so it is
    for them(2)
        that I have worked so hard(5)
            over this drawing.(2)

13. The lesson
    which I pass on(5)
        by this means is worth all the trouble(2)
            (that) it has cost me.(5)

14. Perhaps you will ask me,

15. "Why are there no other drawing
    in this book(2)
        as impressive as this drawing(2, 2)
            of the baobabs?"(2)

16. The reply is simple.
  I have tried.
  But with the others(2)
        I have not been successful.

17. When I made the drawing(5)
    of the baobabs(2)
    I was carried(4)
        beyond myself(2)
        by the urgent necessity.(2)

DAY 17

Step 1 원문 읽기

Oh, little prince! Bit by bit I came to understand the secrets of your sad little life... For a long time you had found your only entertainment in the pleasure of looking at the sunset.

I learned that new detail on the morning of the fourth day, when you said to me:

"I am very fond of sunsets. Come, let us go look at a sunset now."
"But we must wait," I said.
"Wait? For what?"
"For the sunset. We must wait until it is time."

At first you seemed to be very much surprised. And then you laughed to yourself. You said to me:

"I am always thinking that I am at home!"

Just so. Everybody knows that when it is noon in the United States the sun is setting over France.

If you could fly to France in one minute, you could go straight into the sunset, right from noon. Unfortunately, France is too far away for that.

Step 1 원문 읽기

But on your tiny planet, my little prince, all you need to do is move your chair a few steps.[1] You can see the day end and the twilight falling whenever you like...

"One day," you said to me, "I saw the sunset forty-four times!"

And a little later you added:

"You know — one loves the sunset, when one is so sad..."
"Were you so sad, then?" I asked, "on the day of the forty-four sunsets?"

But the little prince made no reply.

---
1. all is (to) move가 (1)입니다.

Step 2 구조 파악과 이해

01. Oh, little prince!
  Bit by bit(2)
    I came
      to understand the secrets(3)
        of your sad little life...(2)

02. For a long time(2)
      you had found your only entertainment
        in the pleasure(2)
          of looking at the sunset.(2, 2)

03. I learned that new detail
      on the morning(2)
        of the fourth day,(2)
          when you said to me:(5, 2)

04. "I am very fond
      of sunsets.(2)
        Come, let us (to) go (to) look
          at a sunset now."(2)

05. "But we must wait," I said.
      "Wait? For what?"

06. "For the sunset.(2)
      We must wait
        until it is time."(5)

07. At first(2)

Step 2 구조 파악과 이해

    you seemed
        to be very much surprised.(3, 4)
   And then you laughed(5)
        to yourself.(2)
   You said to me:(2)

08. "I am always thinking
       that I am at home!"(5)

09. Just so. Everybody knows
      that when it is noon(5)
        in the United States(2)
         the sun is setting
          over France.(2)

10. If you could fly(5)
    to France(2)
      in one minute,(2)
        you could go straight
         into the sunset, right
          from noon.(2)
   Unfortunately, France is too far away
         for that.(2)

11. But on your tiny planet,(2)
    my little prince,
     all (that) you need(5)

Step 2 구조 파악과 이해

　　　　　to do is(3)

　　　　　　(to) move your chair a few steps.(3)

12. You can see the day

　　　　(to) end(3)

　　　　　and the twilight

　　　　　　falling whenever you like...(4, 5)

13. "One day," you said

　　　　　to me,(2)

　　　　　　"I saw the sunset forty-four times!"

And a little later you added:

14. "You know – one loves the sunset,

　　　　　when one is so sad..."(5)

15. "Were you so sad, then?" I asked,

　　　　"on the day(2)

　　　　　of the forty-four sunsets?"(2)

16. But the little prince made no reply.

DAY18

Step 1 원문 읽기

On the fifth day, —always thanks to the sheep —the secret of the little prince's life was revealed. Abruptly, without anything to lead up to it,[1] and as if the question had been born of long and silent meditation on his problem, he demanded:

"A sheep —if it eats little bushes, does it eat flowers, too?"
"A sheep," I answered, "eats anything it finds in its reach."
"Even flowers that have thorns?"
"Yes, even flowers that have thorns."
"Then the thorns —what use are they?"

I didn't know. At that time I was busy trying to unscrew a bolt that had got stuck in my engine. I was very worried, for it was clear to me that the breakdown of my plane was extremely serious. And I had so little drinking-water left that I had to fear for the worst.

"The thorns —what use are they?"

The little prince never let go of a question, once he had asked it. As for me, I was upset over that bolt. And I answered with the first thing that came into my head:

"The thorns are of no use at all. Flowers have thorns just for spite!"
"Oh!"

Step 1 원문 읽기

There was a moment of silence. Then the little prince flashed back at me, with a resentfulness:

"I don't believe you! Flowers are weak creatures. They are naive. They reassure themselves as best they can. They believe that their thorns are terrible weapons..."

I did not answer. At that instant I was saying to myself: "If this bolt still won't turn, I am going to knock it out with the hammer." Again the little prince disturbed my thoughts.

---
1. anything이 lead up 했으니(주제로), 한 주제에 대해 갑자기 말을 꺼냈단 얘기에요.

Step 2 구조 파악과 이해

01. On the fifth day,(2)
　　　－always thanks
　　　　　to the sheep －(2)
　　　　　the secret
　　　　　　　of the little prince's life was revealed.(2, 4)

02. Abruptly,
　　　without anything(2)
　　　　　to lead up to it,(3, 2)

03. and as if the question had been born(5)
　　　　　of long and silent meditation(2)
　　　　　　　on his problem,(2)
　　　　　　　　　he demanded:

04. "A sheep －if it eats little bushes,(5)
　　　　　does it eat flowers, too?"

05. "A sheep," I answered, "eats anything
　　　　　(that) it finds in its reach."(5, 2)

06. "Even flowers
　　　that have thorns?"(5)
　　　　"Yes, even flowers
　　　　　that have thorns."(5)

07. "Then the thorns －what use are they?"

08. I didn't know.
　　　At that time(2)

Step 2 구조 파악과 이해

        I was busy trying
            to unscrew a bolt(3)
                that had got stuck in my engine.(5, 2)

09. I was very worried,
    for it was clear
        to me (2, 2)
            that the breakdown(5)
                of my plane was extremely serious.(2, 4)

10. And I had so little drinking-water
    left that I had(4, 5)
        to fear for the worst.(3, 2)

11. "The thorns — what use are they?"

12. The little prince never let go
    of a question,(2)
        once he had asked it.

13. As for me,(5, 2)
    I was upset
        over that bolt.(2)
    And I answered(5)
        with the first thing(2)
            that came into my head:(5, 2)

14. "The thorns are
    of no use at all.(2)

Step 2 구조 파악과 이해

        Flowers have thorns just
                for spite!"(2)
"Oh!"
15. There was a moment
        of silence.(2)
    Then the little prince flashed back
        at me, with a resentfulness:(2, 2)
16. "I don't believe you!
    Flowers are weak creatures.
    They are naive.
17. They reassure themselves
      as best they can.(5)
    They believe
      that their thorns are terrible weapons..."(5)
18. I did not answer.
    At that instant(2)
      I was saying
        to myself:(2)
19. "If this bolt still won't turn,(5)
      I am going
        to knock it out with the hammer."(3, 2)
20. Again the little prince disturbed
        my thoughts.

DAY 19

Step 1 원문 읽기

"And you actually believe that the flowers –"
"No! I don't believe anything. I answered you with the first thing that came into my head. Don't you see – I am very busy with matters of consequence!"

He stared at me, thunderstruck.

"Matters of consequence!"

He looked at me there, I was bending down over an object which seemed to him extremely ugly. And I was with my hammer in my hand, my fingers black with engine-grease.

"You talk just like the grown-ups!"

That made me a little ashamed. But he went on, relentlessly:[1]

"You mix everything up together... You confuse everything..."

He was really very angry. He tossed his golden curls in the breeze.[2]

"I know a planet where there is a certain red-faced gentleman. He has never smelled a flower. He has never looked at a star. He has never loved any one. He has never done anything in his life but add

Step 1 원문 읽기

up figures. And all day he says over and over, just like you: 'I am busy with matters of consequence!' And that makes him swell up with pride.³ But he is not a man — he is a mushroom!"

"A what?"
"A mushroom!"

The little prince was now white with rage.

"The flowers have been growing thorns for millions of years. For millions of years the sheep have been eating them just the same. And is it not a matter of consequence to try to understand why the flowers make so much trouble? Why the flowers grow thorns which are never of any use to them?

---

1. relentlessly : 단어 뒤에 -ly가 있는 건 대개 부사. 부사는 '~하게' 정도의 뜻. 문장에서 빠져도 큰 지장 없어요.
2. 계속 강조해요! 구조 파악이 먼저입니다. 단어 뜻은 나중에! (toss, curl, breeze... 뜻 몰라도 괜찮다는 얘기에요.)
3. swell도 마찬가지. 저도 처음 보는 단어예요. that makes me laugh / cry / try와 같은 구조!

Step 2   구조 파악과 이해

01. "And you actually believe

      that the flowers —"(5)

02. "No! I don't believe anything.

  I answered you

    with the first thing(2)

      that came into my head.(5)

03. Don't you see —

  I am very busy

    with matters(2)

      of consequence!"(2)

04. He stared

    at me, thunderstruck.(2, 4)

      "Matters of consequence!"(2)

05. He looked

    at me there,(2)

    I was bending down

      over an object(2)

        which seemed(5)

          to him extremely ugly.(2)

06. And I was

    with my hammer(2)

      in my hand,(2)

      my fingers black

Step 2 구조 파악과 이해

        with engine-grease.(2)

07. "You talk just

   like the grown-ups!"(2)

  That made me a little ashamed.

   But he went on, relentlessly:

08. "You mix everything up together...

     You confuse everything..."

09. He was really very angry.

  He tossed his golden curls

    in the breeze.(2)

10. "I know a planet

   where there is(5)

     a certain red-faced gentleman.

     He has never smelled a flower.

11. He has never looked

   at a star.(2)

  He has never loved any one.

12. He has never done anything

    in his life(2)

     but add up figures.(5)

13. And all day he says over and over,

  just like you:(2)

   'I am busy

Step 2 구조 파악과 이해

                  with matters

                        of consequence!'(2, 2)

14. And that makes him

             (to) swell up with pride.(3, 2)

                But he is not a man –

                he is a mushroom!"

15. "A what?"

       "A mushroom!"

   The little prince was now white

                with rage.(2)

16. "The flowers have been growing thorns

                for millions of years.(2)

17. For millions of years

       the sheep have been eating them

                just the same.

18. And isn't it a matter

    of consequence(2)

        to try to understand(3, 3)

            why the flowers make(5)

                so much trouble?

19. Why the flowers grow thorns

    which are never(5)

        of any use to them?(2, 2)

DAY20

Step 1 원문 읽기

Is the warfare between the sheep and the flowers not important?[1] Is this not of more consequence than a fat red-faced gentleman's sums?

And if I know one flower which is unique in the world, which grows nowhere but on my planet, but which one little sheep can destroy in a single bite some morning, without even noticing what he is doing – Oh! You think that is not important!"

His face turned from white to red as he continued:

"If some one loves a flower, of which just one single blossom grows in all the millions of stars. It is enough to make him happy just to look at the stars.

He can say to himself, 'Somewhere, my flower is there…' But if the sheep eats the flower, in one moment all his stars will be darkened… And you think that is not important!"

He could not say anything more. His words were choked by sobbing.[2]

The night had fallen. I had let my tools drop from my hands. Of what moment now was my hammer, my bolt, or thirst, or death?

Step 1 원문 읽기

On one star, one planet, my planet, the Earth, there was a little prince to be comforted. I took him in my arms, and rocked him. I said to him:

"The flower that you love is not in danger. I will draw you a muzzle for your sheep. I will draw you a railing to put around your flower. I will –"

I did not know what to say to him. I felt awkward and blundering. I did not know how I could reach him, and go on hand in hand with him once more.

It is such a secret place, the land of tears.

---
1. the warfare is not important가 기본형 (1).
2. 그가 더 이상 말 안 했다. '그의 단어(말)들은 ~했다 ~에 의해서' 식으로 ~에 맞을 뜻? 단어를 생각해 보는 게 1순위. 그리고 choked, sobbing 이런 단어가 나중에 또 다른 문장에서 나오나 보고, 그 문장에선 뜻이 추측되나 보세요. 그런 식으로 자연스럽게 어휘력을 키워가는 게 제일 좋아요. (우리말도 그렇게 익혔습니다.) 그걸로 부족할 때 사전을 참고하세요.

Step 2   구조 파악과 이해

01. Is the warfare
    between the sheep and the flowers(2)
        not important?

02. Is this not
    of more consequence(2)
        than a fat red-faced gentleman's sums?(2)

03. And if I know one flower(5)
    which is unique(5)
        in the world,(2)
    which grows nowhere(5)
        but on my planet,(2)

04. but which one little sheep can destroy(5)
        in a single bite some morning,(2)

05. without even noticing(2)
    what he is doing —(5)
      Oh! You think
        that is not important!"(5)

06. His face turned
    from white(2)
      to red(2)
        as he continued:(5)

07. "If some one loves a flower,(5)
    of which just one single blossom grows(2, 5)

Step 2   구조 파악과 이해

            in all the millions of stars.(2,2)

08. It is enough

      to make him happy just to look(3,3)

           at the stars.(2)

09. He can say

      to himself,(2)

        'Somewhere, my flower is there...'

10. But if the sheep eats the flower,(5)

      in one moment(2)

        al his stars will be darkened...

11. And you think

      that is not important!"(2)

12. He could not say anything more.

  His words were choked

        by sobbing.(2)

13. The night had fallen.

  I had let my tools

      (to) drop from my hands.(3,2)

14. Of what moment now(2)

      was my hammer, my bolt,

        or thirst, or death?

15. On one star,(2)

      one planet, my planet, the Earth,

Step 2 구조 파악과 이해

there was a little prince
  to be comforted.(3)

16. I took him
  in my arms,(2)
  and rocked him.
  I said
  to him:(2)

17. "The flower
  that you love is not in danger.(5, 2)
  I will draw you a muzzle
    for your sheep.(2)

18. I will draw you a railing
  to put around your flower.(3)

19. I will –" I did not know
  what to say to him.(5, 3, 2)
  I felt awkward and blundering.

20. I did not know
  how I could reach him,(5)
  and go on hand
  in hand with him once more.(2, 2)

21. It is such a secret place, the land
  of tears.(2)

Step 3   3주차 지문을 한 번에 읽어봐요 : DAY 15

There were good plants and bad plants on the planet where the little prince lived – as on all planets. In consequence, there were good seeds from good plants, and bad seeds from bad plants.

But seeds are invisible. They sleep deep in the heart of the earth's darkness. Until some one among them is seized with the desire to awaken. Then this little seed will stretch itself timidly at first. They push a charming little sprig inoffensively upward toward the sun.

If it is only a sprig of radish or rose-bush, one would let it grow wherever it might wish. But when it is a bad plant, one must destroy it as soon as possible, the very first instant that one recognizes it.

Now there were some terrible seeds on the planet that was the home of the little prince; and these were the seeds of the baobab. The soil of that planet was infested with them.

A baobab is something you will never, never be able to get rid of if you attend to it too late. It spreads over the entire planet. It bores clear through it with its roots. And if the planet is too small, and the baobabs are too many, they split it in pieces...

"It is a question of discipline," the little prince said to me later on.

Step 3 3주차 지문을 한 번에 읽어봐요 : DAY 15

"When you've finished your own toilet in the morning, then it is time for your planet for the toilet.

You must see to it that you pull up regularly all the baobabs, at the very first moment when they can be distinguished from the rosebushes. Because they resemble so closely in their earliest youth. It is very tedious work," the little prince added, "but very easy."

Step 3   3주차 지문을 한 번에 읽어봐요 : DAY 16

And one day he said to me: "You ought to make a beautiful drawing, so that the children where you live can see exactly how all this is. That would be very useful to them if they were to travel some day. Sometimes," he added, "there is no harm in putting off a piece of work until another day. But when it is a matter of baobabs, that always means a catastrophe. I knew a planet that was inhabited by a lazy man. He neglected three little bushes..."

So, as the little prince described it to me, I have made a drawing of that planet. I do not like to take the tone of a moralist.

But the danger of the baobabs is so little understood, and such considerable risks would be run by anyone who might get lost on an asteroid, that for once I am breaking through my reserve. "Children," I say, "watch out for the baobabs!"

My friends, like myself, have been skirting this danger for a long time, without ever knowing it; and so it is for them that I have worked so hard over this drawing. The lesson which I pass on by this means is worth all the trouble it has cost me.

Perhaps you will ask me, "Why are there no other drawing in this book as impressive as this drawing of the baobabs?"

Step 3   3주차 지문을 한 번에 읽어봐요 : DAY 16

The reply is simple. I have tried. But with the others I have not been successful. When I made the drawing of the baobabs I was carried beyond myself by the urgent necessity.

Step 3   3주차 지문을 한 번에 읽어봐요 : DAY 17

Oh, little prince! Bit by bit I came to understand the secrets of your sad little life... For a long time you had found your only entertainment in the pleasure of looking at the sunset.

I learned that new detail on the morning of the fourth day, when you said to me:

"I am very fond of sunsets. Come, let us go look at a sunset now."
"But we must wait," I said.
"Wait? For what?"
"For the sunset. We must wait until it is time."

At first you seemed to be very much surprised. And then you laughed to yourself. You said to me:

"I am always thinking that I am at home!"

Just so. Everybody knows that when it is noon in the United States the sun is setting over France.

If you could fly to France in one minute, you could go straight into the sunset, right from noon. Unfortunately, France is too far away for that.

 **Step 3** 3주차 지문을 한 번에 읽어봐요 : DAY 17

But on your tiny planet, my little prince, all you need to do is move your chair a few steps. You can see the day end and the twilight falling whenever you like...

"One day," you said to me, "I saw the sunset forty-four times!"

And a little later you added:

"You know – one loves the sunset, when one is so sad..."
"Were you so sad, then?" I asked, "on the day of the forty-four sunsets?"

But the little prince made no reply.

Step 3 3주차 지문을 한 번에 읽어봐요 : DAY 18

On the fifth day, — always thanks to the sheep — the secret of the little prince's life was revealed. Abruptly, without anything to lead up to it, and as if the question had been born of long and silent meditation on his problem, he demanded:

"A sheep — if it eats little bushes, does it eat flowers, too?"
"A sheep," I answered, "eats anything it finds in its reach."
"Even flowers that have thorns?"
"Yes, even flowers that have thorns."
"Then the thorns — what use are they?"

I didn't know. At that time I was busy trying to unscrew a bolt that had got stuck in my engine. I was very worried, for it was clear to me that the breakdown of my plane was extremely serious. And I had so little drinking-water left that I had to fear for the worst.

"The thorns — what use are they?"

The little prince never let go of a question, once he had asked it. As for me, I was upset over that bolt. And I answered with the first thing that came into my head:

"The thorns are of no use at all. Flowers have thorns just for spite!"
"Oh!"

 **Step 3**   3주차 지문을 한 번에 읽어봐요 : DAY 18

There was a moment of silence. Then the little prince flashed back at me, with a resentfulness:

"I don't believe you! Flowers are weak creatures. They are naive. They reassure themselves as best they can. They believe that their thorns are terrible weapons..."

I did not answer. At that instant I was saying to myself: "If this bolt still won't turn, I am going to knock it out with the hammer." Again the little prince disturbed my thoughts.

Step 3 3주차 지문을 한 번에 읽어봐요 : DAY 19

"And you actually believe that the flowers –"

"No! I don't believe anything. I answered you with the first thing that came into my head. Don't you see – I am very busy with matters of consequence!"

He stared at me, thunderstruck.

"Matters of consequence!"

He looked at me there, I was bending down over an object which seemed to him extremely ugly. And I was with my hammer in my hand, my fingers black with engine-grease.

"You talk just like the grown-ups!"

That made me a little ashamed. But he went on, relentlessly:

"You mix everything up together... You confuse everything..."

He was really very angry. He tossed his golden curls in the breeze.

"I know a planet where there is a certain red-faced gentleman. He has never smelled a flower. He has never looked at a star. He has never loved any one. He has never done anything in his life but add

Step 3   3주차 지문을 한 번에 읽어봐요 : DAY 19

up figures. And all day he says over and over, just like you: 'I am busy with matters of consequence!' And that makes him swell up with pride. But he is not a man —he is a mushroom!"

"A what?"
"A mushroom!"

The little prince was now white with rage.

"The flowers have been growing thorns for millions of years. For millions of years the sheep have been eating them just the same. And is it not a matter of consequence to try to understand why the flowers make so much trouble? Why the flowers grow thorns which are never of any use to them?

Step 3   3주차 지문을 한 번에 읽어봐요 : DAY 20

Is the warfare between the sheep and the flowers not important? Is this not of more consequence than a fat red-faced gentleman's sums?

And if I know one flower which is unique in the world, which grows nowhere but on my planet, but which one little sheep can destroy in a single bite some morning, without even noticing what he is doing – Oh! You think that is not important!"

His face turned from white to red as he continued:

"If some one loves a flower, of which just one single blossom grows in all the millions of stars. It is enough to make him happy just to look at the stars.

He can say to himself, 'Somewhere, my flower is there…' But if the sheep eats the flower, in one moment all his stars will be darkened… And you think that is not important!"

He could not say anything more. His words were choked by sobbing.

The night had fallen. I had let my tools drop from my hands. Of what moment now was my hammer, my bolt, or thirst, or death?

3주차 지문을 한 번에 읽어봐요 : DAY 20

On one star, one planet, my planet, the Earth, there was a little prince to be comforted. I took him in my arms, and rocked him. I said to him:

"The flower that you love is not in danger. I will draw you a muzzle for your sheep. I will draw you a railing to put around your flower. I will –"

I did not know what to say to him. I felt awkward and blundering. I did not know how I could reach him, and go on hand in hand with him once more.

It is such a secret place, the land of tears.

WEEK 4

마지막 4주차! 5구조 적용해서 원서 읽어보기 많이 익숙해졌나요? 계속 강조하지만 구조 파악이 1순위! 우리가 연습하는 문장들이 원문의 레벨과 그다지 다르지 않아요. 아주 조금만 쉽게 만들었으니 스스로 원서 읽고 있단 자부심을 느껴도 좋아요! (실제 원서로 곧 읽어보세요!)

Step 1 원문 읽기

I soon learned to know this flower better. On the little prince's planet the flowers had always been very simple. They had only one ring of petals; they took up no room at all;[1] they were a trouble to nobody. One morning they would appear in the grass, and by night they would have faded peacefully away.

But one day, from a seed blown from no one knew where, a new flower had come up;[2] and the little prince had watched very closely over this small sprout. Because it was not like any other small sprouts on his planet. It might, you see, have been a new kind of baobab.

The shrub soon stopped growing, and began to get ready to produce a flower. The little prince had been present at the first appearance of a huge bud.[3]

He felt at once that some sort of miraculous apparition must emerge from it.[4] But the flower was not satisfied to complete the preparations for her beauty.

She was in the shelter of her green chamber for a long time. She chose her colours with the greatest care. She adjusted her petals one by one. She did not wish to go out into the world all rumpled, like the field poppies.[5]

Step 1 원문 읽기

It was only in the full radiance of her beauty that she wished to appear. Oh, yes! She was a coquettish creature! And her mysterious adornment lasted for days and days.[6]

Then one morning, exactly at sunrise, she suddenly showed herself.

And, after working with all this painstaking precision, she yawned and said:

"Ah! I am scarcely awake. I beg that you will excuse me. My petals are still all disarranged..."

---

1. they took up no room : 자리를 별로 차지 안했다.
2. 'from S (which was) blown from where no one knew.' 정도가 원래 문장.
3. 꽃봉오리가 열리는 현장에 present(있었다) 했다는 뜻.
4. 생소한 단어가 많지만 결국 기본흔은 He felt that some must emerge.
5. rumpled 상태로 세상에 나오고 싶지 않았대요. field poppies처럼. (두 단어 뜻은 저도 모릅니다. 사전 찾으면 나오겠지만 rumpled는 '정리 덜 된' 정도겠고, field poppies는 좀 안 예쁜 꽃이겠죠.) 여러분도 이런 식으로 하면 된다고 저도 같이 하고 있는 거예요.
6. She was C / her M A lasted. 역시 생소한 단어에 겁먹지 마세요. 아주 간단한 문장이네요. 'She was a girl' 'Her beauty Lasted'와 똑같은 (형태의) 문장.

Step 2 구조 파악과 이해

01. I soon learned
    to know this flower better.(3)
02. On the little prince's planet(2)
    the flowers had always been very simple.
03. They had only one ring
    of petals;(2)
        they took up no room at all;
            they were a trouble
                to nobody.(2)
04. One morning they would appear
    in the grass,(2)
        and by night(5, 2)
            they would have faded peacefully away.
05. But one day,
    from a seed blown(2, 4)
        from no one knew where,(5, 2)
            a new flower had come up;
06. and the little prince had watched
    very closely
        over this small sprout.(2)
07. Because it was not
    like any other small sprouts(2)
        on his planet.(2)

Step 2 구조 파악과 이해

08. It might, you see, have been a new kind
                                     of baobab.(2)

09. The shrub soon stopped growing,
         and began
                 to get ready(3)
                         to produce a flower.(3)

10. The little prince had been present
                 at the first appearance(2)
                         of a huge bud.(2)

11. He felt
         at once that some sort(2, 5)
                 of miraculous apparition must emerge(2)
                               from it.(2)

12. But the flower was not satisfied
             to complete the preparations(3)
                     for her beauty.(2)

13. She was
       in the shelter(2)
       of her green chamber(2)
       for a long time.(2)

14. She chose her colours
       with the greatest care.(2)
       She adjusted her petals one

Step 2 구조 파악과 이해

        by one.(2)

15. She did not wish
   to go out(3)
     into the world all rumpled,(3, 4)
      like the field poppies.(2)

16. It was only
   in the full radiance(2)
    of her beauty(2)
     that she wished(5)
      to appear.(3)

17. Oh, yes! She was a coquettish creature!
 And her mysterious adornment lasted
     for days and days.(2)

18. Then one morning, exactly
   at sunrise,(2)
    she suddenly showed herself.

19. And, after working(2, 4)
  with all this painstaking precision,(2)
   she yawned and said:

20. "Ah! I am scarcely awake.
  I beg
   that you will excuse me.(5)
    My petals are still all disarranged…"

DAY 23

Step 1 원문 읽기

But the little prince could not restrain his admiration:

"Oh! How beautiful you are!"
"Am I not?" the flower responded, sweetly. "And I was born at the same moment as the sun…"

The little prince could guess easily enough that she was not any too modest — but how moving — and exciting — she was!

"I think it is time for breakfast," she added an instant later. "If you would have the kindness to think of my needs —"

And the little prince, completely abashed, went to look for a sprinkling-can of fresh water.[1] So, he tended the flower.

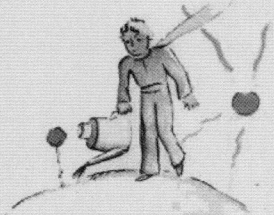

So, she began to torment him with her vanity — which was a little difficult to deal with.[2] One day, for instance, when she was speaking of her four thorns, she said to the little prince:

"Let the tigers come with their claws!"

Step 1 원문 읽기

"There are no tigers on my planet," the little prince objected. "And, anyway, tigers do not eat weeds."

"I am not a weed," the flower replied, sweetly.

"Please excuse me..."

"I am not at all afraid of tigers," she went on, "but I have a horror of drafts. I suppose you wouldn't have a screen for me?"³

"A horror of drafts —that is bad luck, for a plant," remarked the little prince, and added to himself, "This flower is a very complex creature..."

"At night I want you to put me under a glass globe. It is very cold where you live. In the place I came from —"

---

1. prince abashed가 (1)이 아니고 prince went가 (1). 중간에 ','가 구분해 주는 장치인데요. 종종 ',' 가 없는 형태로도 있어요. 직접 다른 원서들 보면서 찾아보세요. ^^
2. 꽃이 자꾸 허영 떨어서 왕자를 피곤하게 했다는 말. 생텍쥐페리가 사랑했던 여성을 꽃으로 묘사한 건 아녔을까요?
3. screen (바람막이, 가리개)가 왜 필요할까를 생각하면 여기서 draft가 뭔지 추측이 되죠.

Step 2 구조 파악과 이해

01. But the little prince could not restrain
       his admiration:
          "Oh! How beautiful you are!"(5)

02. "Am I not?"
    the flower responded, sweetly.
"And I was born
    at the same moment(2)
      as the sun..."(2)

03. The little prince could guess easily enough
    that she was not any too modest —(5)

04. But how moving —
    and exciting — she was!(5)

05. "I think (that) it is time(5)
    for breakfast,"(2)
      she added an instant later.

06. "If you would have the kindness(5)
    to think(3)
      of my needs —"(2)

07. And the little prince,
    completely abashed,(4)
      went to look(3)
        for a sprinkling-can of fresh water.(2, 2)

08. So, he tended the flower.

Step 2 구조 파악과 이해

09. So, she began
    to torment him(3)
        with her vanity —(2)
            which was a little difficult(5)
                to deal with.(3)

10. One day, for instance,(2)
    when she was speaking(5)
        of her four thorns,(2)
        she said
            to the little prince:(2)

11. "Let the tigers
    (to) come with their claws!"(3, 2)

12. "There are no tigers
    on my planet,"(2)
        the little prince objected.
"And, anyway, tigers do not eat weeds."

13. "I am not a weed,"
    the flower replied, sweetly.
"Please excuse me…"

14. "I am not
    at all afraid(2)
        of tigers," she went on,(2)
        "but I have a horror

Step 2 구조 파악과 이해

        of drafts.(2)

15. I suppose

  (that) you wouldn't have a screen(5)

        for me?"(2)

16. "A horror

  of drafts –(2)

    that is bad luck,

      for a plant,"(2)

        remarked the little prince,

         and added(2)

          to himself,

 "This flower is a very complex creature..."

17. "At night I want you

    to put me(3)

      under a glass globe. (2)

 It is very cold

  where you live.(5)

18. In the place(2)

  (that) I came from –"(5)

DAY 24

Step 1 원문 읽기

But she interrupted herself at that point. She had come in the form of a seed. She could not have known anything of any other worlds.

Embarrassed over having let herself be caught on the edge of such an untruth,[1] she coughed two or three times, in order to put the little prince in the wrong.

"The screen?"
"I was just going to look for it when you spoke to me..."

Then she forced her cough a little more so that he should suffer from regret just the same.[2]

So the little prince, in spite of all the good will from his love, had soon come to doubt her.[3] He had taken seriously words which were without importance, and it made him very unhappy.[4]

"I ought not to have listened to her," he confided to me one day. "One should simply look at them and breathe their fragrance. Mine perfumed all my planet.[5] But I did not know how to take pleasure in all her grace. This tale of claws, which disturbed me so much, should only have filled my heart with pity."[6]

And he continued his confidences:

Step 1 원문 읽기

"The fact is that I did not know how to understand anything! I ought to have judged by deeds and not by words.[7] She cast her fragrance and her radiance over me. I ought never to have run away from her... I ought to have guessed all the affection that lay behind her poor little means.[8] Flowers are so inconsistent! But I was too young to know how to love her..."

생소한 단어(영어 문제)가 있기도 하지만, 내용 자체가 약간 어려워요. 이해력 문제이지 영어 문제가 아니란 것).
1. ① 이 문장에서 주어+동사는 뭘까요? ② let herself (to) be : 여러 번 했죠? ③ on the edge of an untruth : 안 진실함의 edge니, 꽃의 과장이 너무 심했단 얘기.
2. he suffer from regret : 왕자를 더 미안하게 만들려고 했단 얘기.
3. prince had come to doubt her. 결론은 이 정도.
4. words without importance : 안 중요한 말들.
5. Mine perfumed all my planet!! 'I like you'와 동일 형태의 다주 단순한 문장. 그런데 뜻이 정말 예쁘네요!
6. Tale should have filled with pity. 꽃의 가시 이야기를 그냥 안쓰럽게 들어줬으면 됐다는 얘기. (계속 단순 영어 문제가 아니라, 좀 말 자체가 약간 어려워요.)
7. 명언이네요. What a great line!
8. I have to guess AFFECTION that behind her bad behaviors. 그녀의 성가신 행동 뒤의 애정을 알아 봤어야!

분명 저 꽃에 대한 생각은 생텍쥐페리가 사랑했던 여성과의 경험에서 나 온 거라 생각해요. 남자 여러분! 여자들이 틱틱 거려도 그냥 예쁘다 해줍시다!! 여자 여러분! 남자들이 허세 부려도 그 냥 귀엽게 봐주세요. ^^

Step 2   구조 파악과 이해

01. But she interrupted herself
       at that point.(2)
    She had come
       in the form of a seed.(2, 2)

02. She could not have known anything
       of any other worlds.(2)

03. Embarrassed(4)
       over having let herself(2)
          (to) be caught(3)
             on the edge of such an untruth.(2, 2)

04. she coughed two or three times,
       in order(2)
          to put the little prince(2)
             in the wrong.(2)

05. "The screen?"
    "I was just going
       to look for it(2, 2)
          when you spoke to me..."(5, 2)

06. Then she forced her cough a little more
       so that he should suffer(5)
          from regret just the same.(2)

07. So the little prince,
       in spite(2)

Step 2 구조 파악과 이해

    of all the good will.(2)

   from his love,(2)

  had soon come

   to doubt her.(3)

08. He had taken seriously words

  which were(5)

   without importance,(2)

    and it made him very unhappy.

09. "I ought not

  to have listened to her,"(3, 2)

   he confided

    to me one day.(2)

10. One should simply look

  at them(2)

   and breathe their fragrance.

 Mine perfumed all my planet.

11. But I did not know

  how to take pleasure(5, 3)

   in all her grace.(2)

12. This tale

 of claws,(2)

 which disturbed me so much,(5)

  should only have filled my heart

Step 2 구조 파악과 이해

with pity."(2)

13. And he continued his confidences:

14. "The fact is
    that I did not know(5)
    how to understand anything!(5, 3)

15. I ought
    to have judged(3)
    by deeds and not by words.(2)

16. She cast her fragrance and her radiance
    over me.(2)
    I ought never
    to have run away(3)
    from her...(2)

17. I ought
    to have guessed all the affection(3)
    that lay(5)
    behind her poor little means.(2)

18. Flowers are so inconsistent!
    But I was too young
    to know(3)
    how to love her..."(5, 3)

DAY25

Step 1 원문 읽기

I believe that for his escape he took advantage of the migration of a flock of wild birds.[1] On the morning of his departure he put his planet in perfect order.

He carefully cleaned out his active volcanoes. He possessed two active volcanoes; and they were very convenient for heating his breakfast in the morning.

He also had one volcano that was extinct. But, as he said, "One never knows!" So he cleaned out the extinct volcano, too. If they are well cleaned out, volcanoes burn slowly and steadily, without any eruptions. Volcanic eruptions are like fires in a chimney.

On our earth we are obviously much too small to clean out our volcanoes. That is why they bring no end of trouble upon us.[2]

The little prince also pulled up, with a sense of melancholy, the last little shoots of the baobabs.[3] He believed that he would never want to return. But on this last morning all these familiar tasks seemed very precious to him.

He watered the flower for the last time, and place her under the shelter of her glass globe. And he realised that he was very close to tears.

Step 1 원문 읽기

"Goodbye," he said to the flower.

But she made no answer.

"Goodbye," he said again.

The flower coughed. But it was not because she had a cold.

"I have been silly," she said to him, at last. "I ask your forgiveness. Try to be happy..."

He was surprised by this absence of blame.[4] He stood there all bewildered,[5] the glass globe held arrested in mid-air. He did not understand this quiet sweetness.

---

1. I believe that he took advantage of the ~~~
2. they bring no end : no end를 bring하니까 '끝없는'.
3. prince pulled the shoots가 (1).
4. absence of blame : 비난의 부재(없음). 꽃이 뭐라고 안 해서 왕자가 놀랐다는 것.
5. bewildered : 사전 뜻 찾기보다, 그래서 어린 왕자가 어떻게 서 있었을까요?

Step 2 구조 파악과 이해

01. I believe that(5)
　　　for his escape(2)
　　　　　he took advantage
　　　　　　　of the migration(2)
　　　　　　　　　of a flock(2)
　　　　　　　　　　　of wild birds.(2)
02. On the morning(2)
　　　of his departure(2)
　　　he put his planet
　　　　　in perfect order.(2)
03. He carefully cleaned out
　　　his active volcanoes.
　　　　　He possessed two active volcanoes;
04. and they were very convenient
　　　for heating his breakfast(2)
　　　　　in the morning.(2)
05. He also had one volcano
　　　that was extinct.(5)
　　　　　But, as he said, "One never knows!"
06. So he cleaned out
　　　the extinct volcano, too.
07. If they are well cleaned out,(5)
　　　volcanoes burn slowly and steadily,

Step 2 구조 파악과 이해

without any eruptions.(2)

08. Volcanic eruptions are

　　like fires in a chimney.(2, 2)

09. On our earth(2)

　　we are obviously much too small

　　　　to clean out our volcanoes.(3)

10. That is

　　why they bring no end(5)

　　　　of trouble upon us.(2, 2)

11. The little prince also pulled up,

　　with a sense of melancholy,(2, 2)

　　　　the last little shoots

　　　　　　of the baobabs.(2)

12. He believed

　　that he would never want(5)

　　　　to return.(3)

13. But on this last morning(2)

　　all these familiar tasks seemed

　　　　very precious

　　　　　　to him.(2)

14. He watered the flower

　　for the last time,(2)

　　　　and place her

Step 2 구조 파악과 이해

        under the shelter of her glass globe.(2, 2)

15. And he realised

    that he was very close

        to tears.(3)

16. "Goodbye," he said

        to the flower. (2)

        But she made no answer.

        "Goodbye," he said again.

17. The flower coughed.

    But it was not

        because she had a cold.(5)

18. "I have been silly,"

    she said

        to him, at last.(2)

"I ask your forgiveness. Try

        to be happy..."(3)

19. He was surprised

    by this absence of blame.(2, 2)

20. He stood there all bewildered,(4)

    the glass globe held arrested(4)

        in mid-air.(2)

21. He did not understand

    this quiet sweetness.

DAY 26

Step 1 원문 읽기

"Of course I love you," the flower said. "It is my fault that you have not known it all the while.¹ That is of no importance. But you —you have been just as foolish as I. Try to be happy... let the glass globe be. I don't want it any more."
"But the wind —"
"My cold is not so bad as all that... the cool night air will do me good. I am a flower."
"But the animals —"
"I must endure the presence of some caterpillars if I wish to become acquainted with the butterflies. It seems that they are very beautiful. And if not the butterflies, who will call on me? You will be far away... as for the large animals —I am not at all afraid of any of them. I have my claws."

And, naively, she showed her four thorns. Then she added:

"Don't linger like this.² You have decided to go away. Now go!"

For she did not want him to see her crying. She was such a proud flower...

He found himself in the neighborhood of the asteroids 325, 326, 327, 328, 329, and 330. He began, therefore, by visiting them, in order to add to his knowledge.

Step 1 원문 읽기

The first of them was inhabited by a king. Clad in royal purple and ermine,[3] he was seated upon a throne which was at the same time both simple and majestic.

"Ah! Here is a subject," exclaimed the king, when he saw the little prince coming.

And the little prince asked himself:

"How could he recognize me when he had never seen me before?"

He did not know how the world is simplified for kings. To them, all men are subjects.

---

1. 'you have not known it.' It is that the flower loves him. 꽃이 계속 틱틱 거려서, 자기가 좋아하는 걸 왕자가 몰랐을 거고, 그건 자기 잘못이란 말.
2. linger는 stay 정도. 물론 뜻 몰라도 구조 파악 가능! ① 여기서 있지 마. ② 여기서 먹지 마. ③ 여기서 사색하지 마. 외국인이 보면 ③이 어렵겠지만 결국 구조는 같단 것. 단어 뜻 모른다고 괜히 겁먹지 말고 구조 파악하며 원서를 읽어나가자는 것! 계속 강조해온 이 책의 핵심이에요.
3. purple and ermine이 뭔지 몰라도 암튼 왕이 purple and ermine 안에 있는 걸(입고 있다) 생각하면 돼요.

Step 2 구조 파악과 이해

01. "Of course(2)
  I love you." the flower said.
 "It is my fault
  that you have not known it
   all the while.(5)

02. That is
  of no importance.(2)
   But you — you have been just
    as foolish as I.(2)
     Try
      to be happy...(3)

03. let the glass globe
  (to) be.(3)
   I don't want it any more."
 "But the wind —"

04. "My cold is not so bad
  as all that...(2)
   the cool night air will do me good.
    I am a flower."

05. "But the animals —"

06. "I must endure the presence
  of some caterpillars if I wish(2, 5)
   to become acquainted(3, 4)

Step 2 구조 파악과 이해

　　　　　　　　　　with the butterflies.(2)

07. It seems
　　　that they are very beautiful.(5)
　　　And if not the butterflies,(5)
　　　　　　who will call on me?(5, 2)

08. You will be far away...
　　　as for the large animals —(2)
　　　　　am not
　　　　　　at all afraid of any of them.(2, 2, 2)

09. I have my claws."
　　　And, naively, she showed her four thorns.
　　　Then she added:

10. "Don't linger
　　　like this.(2)
　　　　You have decided
　　　　　　to go away.(3)
　　　　　　Now go!"

11. For she did not want him
　　　to see her crying.(3)
　　　　She was such a proud flower...

12. He found himself
　　　in the neighborhood(2)
　　　　of the asteroids 325(2)

Step 2 구조 파악과 이해

      326, 327, 328, 329, and 330.
13. He began, therefore,
  by visiting them, in order(2, 2)
    to add to his knowledge.(2)
14. The first
  of them(2)
    was inhabited by a king.(4, 2)
 Clad
  in royal purple and ermine,(2)
15. he was seated(4)
  upon a throne(2)
    which was at the same time(5, 2)
      both simple and majestic.
16. "Ah! Here is a subject,"
  exclaimed the king,
    when he saw the little prince coming.(5)
17. And the little prince asked himself:
18. "How could he recognize me
  when he had never seen me before?"(5)
19. He did not know
  how the world is simplified for kings.(5, 2)
 To them,(2)
  all men are subjects.

DAY 27

Step 1 원문 읽기

"Approach, so that I may see you better," said the king, who felt consumingly proud of being at last a king over somebody.[1]

The little prince looked everywhere to find a place to sit down; but the entire planet was crammed and obstructed by the king's magnificent ermine robe.[2] So he remained standing upright, and, since he was tired, he yawned.

"It is contrary to etiquette to yawn in the presence of a king," the monarch said to him. "I forbid you to do so."
"I can't help it. I can't stop myself," replied the little prince, thoroughly embarrassed. "I have come on a long journey, and I have had no sleep…"

"Ah, then," the king said. "I order you to yawn. It is years since I have seen anyone yawning. Yawns, to me, are objects of curiosity.[3] Come, now! Yawn again! It is an order."
"That frightens me… I cannot, any more…" murmured the little prince, now completely abashed.[4]
"Hum! Hum!" replied the king. "Then I —I order you sometimes to yawn and sometimes to —"

He sputtered a little, and seemed vexed.[5]

Step 1 원문 읽기

For what the king fundamentally insisted upon was that his authority should be respected.[6] He tolerated no disobedience. He was an absolute monarch. But, because he was a very good man, he made his orders reasonable.

"If I ordered a general," he would say, by way of example, "if I ordered a general to change himself into a sea bird, and if the general did not obey me, that would not be the fault of the general. It would be my fault."

"May I sit down?" came now a timid inquiry from the little prince.[7]

---

1. 더 간략히 하면 who felt proud (5) of being a king (2, 4) over somebody (2).
2. planet was C—ed and O—ed by K's M E R. 단어는 생소해도 아주 기본형 문장. 'I was tired by it'과 같은 형태.
3. Yawns are objects. (1)
4. the prince murmured, abashed. '왕자는 murmured 했다 abashed 상태로'의 구조
5. sputtered, vexed. 제가 적지 않은 원서 읽었음에도 처음 보는 단어입니다. (물론 원서 더 읽기도 해야겠죠.) 하지만 요즘은, 계속 말하듯 구조를 먼저 보라는 것! 'He studied and seemed tired'와 같은 형태잖아요. 그 상태에서 한국어도 그렇게 익혀왔듯, 앞뒤 문맥을 맞춰 단어 뜻을 추측하는 거죠. 왕이 어린 왕자에게 하품하라고 명령했지만, 하품을 안 할 수도, 할 수도 없는 애매한 상황이면 왕이 어떨까요?
6. 여기서 for는 because입니다. for what was that = for you were my son.
7. a timid inquiry came from the prince.

Step 2 구조 파악과 이해

01. "Approach,
  so that I may see you better,"(5)
    said the king,
      who felt consumingly proud(5)
        of being(2, 4)
          at last a king(2)
            over somebody.(2)

02. The little prince looked everywhere
    to find a place to sit down;(3, 3)

03. but the entire planet was
    crammed and obstructed(4)
      by the king's magnificent ermine robe.(2)

04. So he remained standing upright,(4)
  and, since he was tired,(5, 4)
    he yawned.

05. "It is contrary
  to etiquette to yawn(2, 3)
    in the presence of a king,"(2, 2)
      the monarch said to him.(2)

06. "I forbid you
  to do so."(3)

07. "I can't help it. I can't stop myself,"
    replied the little prince,

218

Step 2 구조 파악과 이해

       thoroughly embarrassed.(4)

08. "I have come

  on a long journey,(2)

    and I have had no sleep…"

09. "Ah, then," the king said.

 "I order you

   to yawn.(3)

    It is years

     since I have seen anyone(5)

       yawning.(4)

10. Yawns, to me,(2)

  are objects

   of curiosity.(2)

    Come, now!

    Yawn again!

     It is an order."

11. "That frightens me…

  I cannot, any more…"

   murmured the little prince,

    now completely abashed.(4)

12. "Hum! Hum!" replied the king.

 "Then I – I order you sometimes

   to yawn and sometimes to –"(3)

Step 2 구조 파악과 이해

13. He sputtered a little, and seemed
                                                      vexed.(4)

14. For what the king fundamentally insisted upon was(5)
                        that his authority should be(5)
                                      respected.(4)

15. He tolerated no disobedience.
              He was an absolute monarch.

16. But, because he was a very good man,
              he made his orders reasonable.

17. "If I ordered a general,"(5)
            he would say,
               by way of example,(2, 2)

18. "if I ordered a general(5)
        to change himself(3)
            into a sea bird,(2)
              and if the general did not obey me,(5)
                that would not be the fault(5)
                  of the general.(2)
                    It would be my fault."

19. "May I sit down?"
        came now a timid inquiry
            from the little prince.(2)

DAY28

Step 3   4주차 지문을 한 번에 읽어봐요 : DAY 22

I soon learned to know this flower better. On the little prince's planet the flowers had always been very simple. They had only one ring of petals; they took up no room at all; they were a trouble to nobody. One morning they would appear in the grass, and by night they would have faded peacefully away.

But one day, from a seed blown from no one knew where, a new flower had come up; and the little prince had watched very closely over this small sprout. Because it was not like any other small sprouts on his planet. It might, you see, have been a new kind of baobab.

The shrub soon stopped growing, and began to get ready to produce a flower. The little prince had been present at the first appearance of a huge bud.

He felt at once that some sort of miraculous apparition must emerge from it. But the flower was not satisfied to complete the preparations for her beauty.

She was in the shelter of her green chamber for a long time. She chose her colours with the greatest care. She adjusted her petals one by one. She did not wish to go out into the world all rumpled, like the field poppies.

4주차 지문을 한 번에 읽어봐요 : DAY 22

It was only in the full radiance of her beauty that she wished to appear. Oh, yes! She was a coquettish creature! And her mysterious adornment lasted for days and days.

Then one morning, exactly at sunrise, she suddenly showed herself.

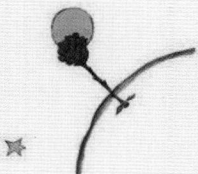

And, after working with all this painstaking precision, she yawned and said:

"Ah! I am scarcely awake. I beg that you will excuse me. My petals are still all disarranged..."

But the little prince could not restrain his admiration:

"Oh! How beautiful you are!"
"Am I not?" the flower responded, sweetly. "And I was born at the same moment as the sun..."

The little prince could guess easily enough that she was not any too modest – but how moving – and exciting – she was!

"I think it is time for breakfast," she added an instant later. "If you would have the kindness to think of my needs –"

And the little prince, completely abashed, went to look for a sprinkling-can of fresh water. So, he tended the flower.

So, she began to torment him with her vanity – which was a little difficult to deal with. One day, for instance, when she was speaking of her four thorns, she said to the little prince:

"Let the tigers come with their claws!"

Step 3 4주차 지문을 한 번에 읽어봐요 : DAY 23

"There are no tigers on my planet," the little prince objected. "And, anyway, tigers do not eat weeds."

"I am not a weed," the flower replied, sweetly.

"Please excuse me..."

"I am not at all afraid of tigers," she went on, "but I have a horror of drafts. I suppose you wouldn't have a screen for me?"

"A horror of drafts—that is bad luck, for a plant," remarked the little prince, and added to himself, "This flower is a very complex creature..."

"At night I want you to put me under a glass globe. It is very cold where you live. In the place I came from —"

Step 3   4주차 지문을 한 번에 읽어봐요 : DAY 24

But she interrupted herself at that point. She had come in the form of a seed. She could not have known anything of any other worlds.

Embarrassed over having let herself be caught on the edge of such an untruth, she coughed two or three times, in order to put the little prince in the wrong.

"The screen?"
"I was just going to look for it when you spoke to me…"

Then she forced her cough a little more so that he should suffer from regret just the same.

So the little prince, in spite of all the good will from his love, had soon come to doubt her. He had taken seriously words which were without importance, and it made him very unhappy.

"I ought not to have listened to her," he confided to me one day. "One should simply look at them and breathe their fragrance. Mine perfumed all my planet. But I did not know how to take pleasure in all her grace. This tale of claws, which disturbed me so much, should only have filled my heart with pity."

And he continued his confidences:

4주차 지문을 한 번에 읽어봐요 : DAY 24

"The fact is that I did not know how to understand anything! I ought to have judged by deeds and not by words. She cast her fragrance and her radiance over me. I ought never to have run away from her… I ought to have guessed all the affection that lay behind her poor little means. Flowers are so inconsistent! But I was too young to know how to love her…"

Step 3 4주차 지문을 한 번에 읽어봐요 : DAY 25

I believe that for his escape he took advantage of the migration of a flock of wild birds. On the morning of his departure he put his planet in perfect order.

He carefully cleaned out his active volcanoes. He possessed two active volcanoes; and they were very convenient for heating his breakfast in the morning.

He also had one volcano that was extinct. But, as he said, "One never knows!" So he cleaned out the extinct volcano, too. If they are well cleaned out, volcanoes burn slowly and steadily, without any eruptions. Volcanic eruptions are like fires in a chimney.

On our earth we are obviously much too small to clean out our volcanoes. That is why they bring no end of trouble upon us.

The little prince also pulled up, with a sense of melancholy, the last little shoots of the baobabs. He believed that he would never want to return. But on this last morning all these familiar tasks seemed very precious to him.

He watered the flower for the last time, and place her under the shelter of her glass globe. And he realised that he was very close to tears.

Step 3   4주차 지문을 한 번에 읽어봐요 : DAY 25

"Goodbye," he said to the flower.

But she made no answer.

"Goodbye," he said again.

The flower coughed. But it was not because she had a cold.

"I have been silly," she said to him, at last. "I ask your forgiveness. Try to be happy .."

He was surprised by this absence of blame. He stood there all bewildered, the glass globe held arrested in mid-air. He did not understand this quiet sweetness.

Step 3   4주차 지문을 한 번에 읽어봐요 : DAY 26

"Of course I love you," the flower said. "It is my fault that you have not known it all the while. That is of no importance. But you — you have been just as foolish as I. Try to be happy… let the glass globe be. I don't want it any more."

"But the wind —"

"My cold is not so bad as all that… the cool night air will do me good. I am a flower."

"But the animals —"

"I must endure the presence of some caterpillars if I wish to become acquainted with the butterflies. It seems that they are very beautiful. And if not the butterflies, who will call on me? You will be far away… as for the large animals — I am not at all afraid of any of them. I have my claws."

And, naively, she showed her four thorns. Then she added:

"Don't linger like this. You have decided to go away. Now go!"

For she did not want him to see her crying. She was such a proud flower…

He found himself in the neighborhood of the asteroids 325, 326, 327, 328, 329, and 330. He began, therefore, by visiting them, in order to add to his knowledge.

Step 3 4주차 지문을 한 번에 읽어봐요 : DAY 26

The first of them was inhabited by a king. Clad in royal purple and ermine, he was seated upon a throne which was at the same time both simple and majestic.

"Ah! Here is a subject," exclaimed the king, when he saw the little prince coming.

And the little prince asked himself:

"How could he recognize me when he had never seen me before?"

He did not know how the world is simplified for kings. To them, all men are subjects.

Step 3 4주차 지문을 한 번에 읽어봐요 : DAY 27

"Approach, so that I may see you better," said the king, who felt consumingly proud of being at last a king over somebody.

The little prince looked everywhere to find a place to sit down; but the entire planet was crammed and obstructed by the king's magnificent ermine robe. So he remained standing upright, and, since he was tired, he yawned.

"It is contrary to etiquette to yawn in the presence of a king," the monarch said to him. "I forbid you to do so."
"I can't help it. I can't stop myself," replied the little prince, thoroughly embarrassed. "I have come on a long journey, and I have had no sleep..."

"Ah, then," the king said. "I order you to yawn. It is years since I have seen anyone yawning. Yawns, to me, are objects of curiosity. Come, now! Yawn again! It is an order."
"That frightens me... I cannot, any more..." murmured the little prince, now completely abashed.
"Hum! Hum!" replied the king. "Then I – I order you sometimes to yawn and sometimes to –"

He sputtered a little, and seemed vexed.

Step 3 4주차 지문을 한 번에 읽어봐요 : DAY 27

For what the king fundamentally insisted upon was that his authority should be respected. He tolerated no disobedience. He was an absolute monarch. But, because he was a very good man, he made his orders reasonable.

"If I ordered a general," he would say, by way of example, "if I ordered a general to change himself into a sea bird, and if the general did not obey me, that would not be the fault of the general. It would be my fault."
"May I sit down?" came now a timid inquiry from the little prince.

책을 마치며...

정말 수고 많았어요! 이제 막 어린 왕자가 본격적으로 여행에 들어가는 부분인데 끝나서 아쉽네요. 더 익숙해질 때까지 이 책으로 반복해서 복습해도 좋고요. 얘기했다시피 원문《어린 왕자》에서 아주 조금만 쉽게 리라이팅 했으니, 실제 원서에 도전해서 나머지 내용을 확인해봐도 좋을 거예요. 기본 전치사와 동사를 잘 익혀두고, 구조 파악 잘 해가며 원서를 많이 읽다 보면 점점 감이 올 겁니다.

저도 어릴 때《어린 왕자》를 한글로 읽어보고, 대게 그렇듯(?) 어디선가 찾은 원서를 읽어보려다 1~2페이지를 못 넘기고 포기했던 기억이 나요. 그리고 언젠간 원서로 읽어봐야지... 하면서도 잘 안 됐는데, 영어 학습법 책 300여권을 읽어보고 많은 영어 고수들을 연구하고, 그래도 방법이 안 나와서 한참을 고민하다 찾아낸 방법이 지금 여러분이 연습하고 있는 방법이에요.

이 책을 내기 전 이미 5년간 임상 실험(?)을 마쳤어요. (실제로 많은 원서를 읽어보면서 적용이 잘 되는지 확인해봤단 얘기예요.) 여러분도 이 방법으로 계속해보면 문법 전혀 몰라도, 좀 생소한 단어가 있어도 원서를 읽을 수 있단 걸 알게 될 거예요. 그럼 사람들 많은 데서 원서 들고 다니면서 폼 좀 잡아보세요. ^^ 물론 저처럼 '진짜가 될 때까지 진짜인 척' 해도 됩니다. (전 못 읽었지만, 자꾸 원서를 들고 읽는 척을 했어요.)

이 책 쓰느라 정말 많은 연구와 생각을 했는데 막상 너무 간단해진 것 같아 좀 당황스럽네요. 그래도 이 책으로 연습해서 쉽게 원서 읽는 분들 보면 기분이 좋습니다. 여러분도 포기하지 말고 꾸준히 연습해서 원서 술술 읽으세요!

부록

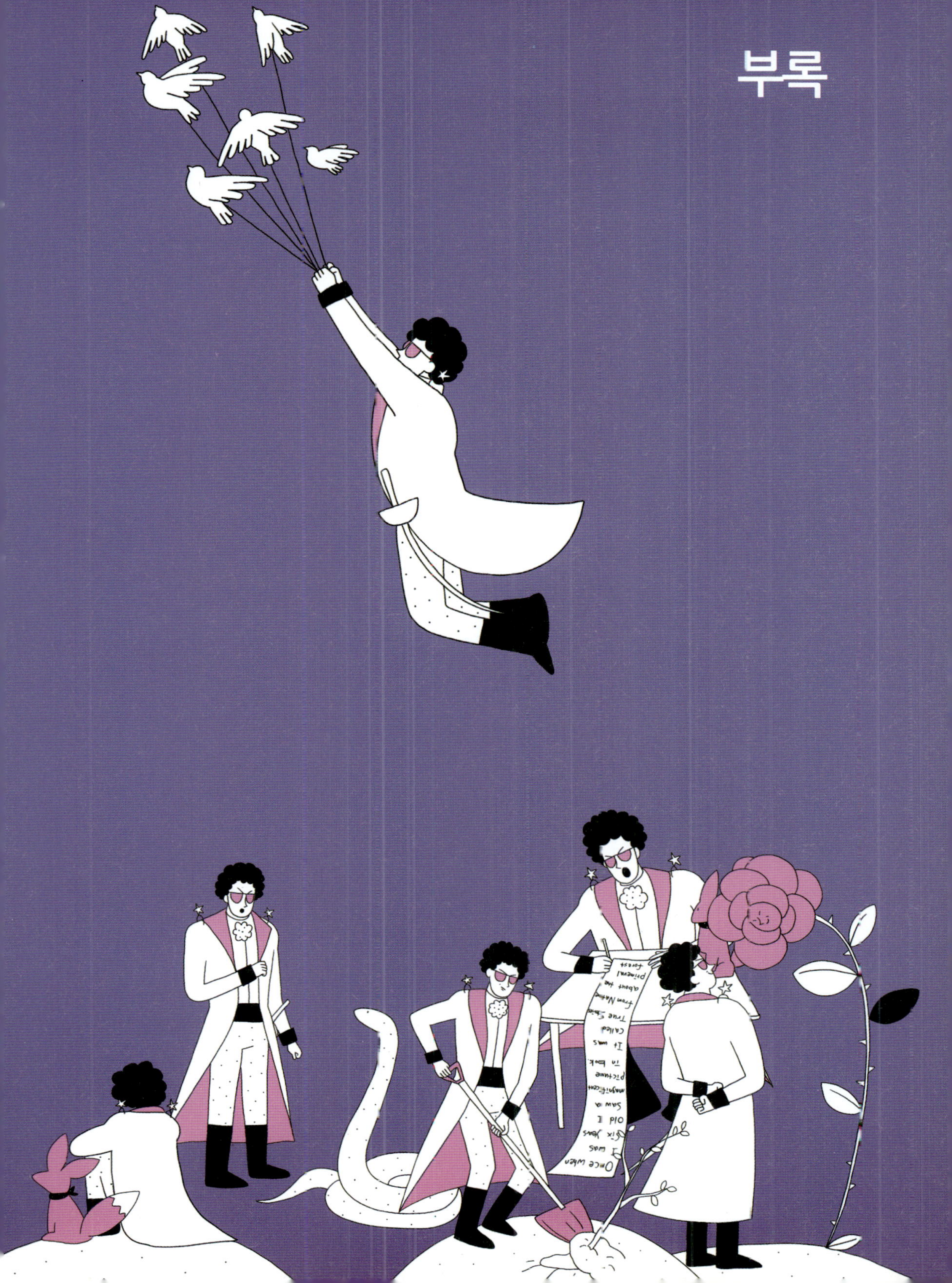
Once when
I was
Six years
old I
Saw a
magnificent
picture
in book.
It was
Called
True
from
about the
primeval
forest

출처: 두산백과

앙투안 드 생텍쥐페리
(Antoine de Saint-Exupéry, 1900~1944)

리옹(Lyons) 출생. 옛 귀족 집안에서 태어나 행복한 어린 시절을 보냈으며, 1920년 징병으로 공군에 입대하여 조종사 훈련을 받았다. 제대 후 자동차 공장 등 여러 직종을 전전하다가, 평범한 사회의 일상생활에서 벗어나 행동적인 인생을 개척하고자 1926년부터 위험이 뒤따르는 초기 우편비행 사업에 가담하였다. 제2차 세계대전이 일어나자 군용기 조종사로 종군, 대전 말기에 정찰비행 중 행방불명이 되었다.

최초의 본격적인 작품《남방 우편기 Courrier Sud》(1929)에서 유작(遺作)《성채(城砦) Citadelle》(1948)에 이르는 모든 작품은 행동을 통한 명상에서 비롯된 것으로, 언제나 어려움과 역경과의 싸움에서 인간이 삶을 영위해 나가는 의의를 찾아 내놓은 것이라고 할 수 있다. 아르헨티나 항공에 근무하던 시기의 경험을 토대로 한《야간비행 Vol de nuit》(1931)은 행동적인 문학으로서 A. 지드의 격찬을 받았으며 페미나상(賞)을 받았다.

그가 추구한 진정한 의미의 삶은 개개의 인간 존재가 아니라, 개적(個的) 존재를 초월한, 즉 사람과 사람을 맺어주는 정신적 유대에서 찾으려 했다는 데 있다.《인간의 대지 Terre des hommes》(1939)《전투 조종사 Pilote de guerre》(1942)에서는 이러한 그의 관점에서 인간의 관계와 동료 비행사, 그리고 임무·의무·조국 등에 관한 문제에 대하여 깊은 성찰이 이루어지고 있다. 제2차 세계대전 중 미국에서 발표한《어린 왕자 Le Petit Prince》(1943)는 작가 자신이 아름다운 삽화를 넣어서 독특한 시적 세계를 이루고 있다.

출처: 서양의 고전을 읽는다, 2006, 휴머니스트

어린 왕자
(The Little Prince, 1943)

밖으로부터의 성찰

《어린 왕자》는 비행기 기관 고장으로 사하라 사막에 불시착한 비행사가 소혹성 B612호에서 왔다는 어린 왕자를 만나, 그와 나눈 이야기와 행동을 기록한 작품이다. 비행사는 어린 시절 코끼리를 삼키고 있는 보아 뱀 그림을 그려서 어른들에게 보여준 적이 있다. 그러나 어른들은 그 그림에서 보아 뱀을 보지 못한 채 모자 형상만을 볼 따름이었다. 어린이에 비해 어른들이 얼마나 본질적인 것을 잘 보지 못하는가를 일찌감치 체험했던 것이다.

그 어린이가 그림에 대한 꿈을 접고 이제 비행사 어른이 되어 있다. 양 한 마리만 그려달라는 어린 왕자의 부탁을 받고 그림을 그려주는 과정에서 비행사는 자신도 어느덧 어린 시절 자기 그림을 제대로 보아주지 못했던 어른들과 닮아 있음을 절감하면서 반성하게 된다. 그렇게 어린 왕자를 알아가게 된다. 이야기는 소혹성에서 어린 왕자의 생활, 지구에 오기 전까지 어린 왕자의 별 여행기, 지구에서의 여정을 담고 있으며, 1년 만에 어린 왕자가 죽어 사라지는 것으로 전개된다.

일차적으로 《어린 왕자》는 지구 바깥에서 온 어린 왕자의 독특한 시선과 행동으로 독자들의 관심을 끌기에 충분하다. 바깥의 시선과 사유를 통해서 지구 안에서 살아가는 어른들의 삶에 대한 반성적 성찰을 유도하고 있는 텍스트이다. 일상적인 삶의 억압과 의무, 경쟁적 현실에서 살아남기 등 여러모로 어른들은 어린 시절에 꾸었던 순정한 꿈과는 다르게 소외된 삶을 억지로 살아가는 경우가 많다. 꿈의 근원으로부터 멀어진 채 고립과 소외의 늪에서 때때로 진실하지 않은 방법으로 자기 삶뿐만 아니라 남들의 삶도 일그러뜨릴 수 있다. 진정한 인간관계가 아득해질 뿐만 아니라 개개인은 존재 가치로부터 멀어지기 일쑤이다.

그러기에 삶의 진정한 가치를 갈구하는 개인들은 영혼의 별자리를 동경하게 되고, 그러면서 프루스트가 그랬듯이 '잃어버린 시간을 찾아서' 방황하고 탐색하게 마련이다. 그러니까 생텍쥐페리의 《어린 왕자》는 잃어버린 시간, 잃어버린 공간, 잃어버린 존재를 찾아서 진정한 인간 영혼의 성장을 모색한 소설이라 할 수 있다.

그토록 이상한 어른들의 세계

이 소설에서 화자는 어린 왕자가 "당신은 마치 어른 같은 말을 하는군!" 하고 말할 때마다 부끄러움을 느낀다. 그렇다면 부끄러움의 대상이 되는 어른의 세계, 다시 말해 본질적인 것을 잃어버린 어른들의 삶의 실상은 어떠한가. 어린 왕자는 자신이 알고 있는 어느 별의 검붉은 얼굴을 한 신사 이야기를 한다.

> 그 분은 아무도 사랑한 일도 없었고, 일상 하고 있는 일이란 덧셈뿐이야. 그리고 그는 날이면 날마다 당신처럼 '나는 중요한 일로 바쁘단 말이야'라고 입버릇처럼 되풀이하고 또 되풀이하지. 그리고는 그 말이 무슨 자랑인 양 뽐내기만 하거든.

이 신사처럼 어른들은 늘 덧셈을 하느라 바쁘다. 덧셈이란 무엇일까. 사랑이 결여된 욕망의 덧셈일 수 있다. 권력, 명예, 재산 등을 보태려는 욕망의 덧셈 말이다. 뿐만 아니다. 어린 왕자가 자신의 소혹성을 떠나 여행했다는 몇몇 별들에서 만난 어른들의 이야기들에서 어른들의 세계는 비판적 성찰의 대상이 된다.

첫 번째 별에는 왕이 살고 있었다. 모든 존재를 자기 신하로 삼고 싶어 하는 권력의 화신이다. 금지와 허용, 지배와 명령을 통해 모든 존재들이 자기에게 복종하도록 하려 한다. 두 번째 별에는 허영심이 많은 독단자가 살고 있었다. 그는 자신을 칭찬하고 찬미

하는 말 이외에는 들을 줄 몰랐다. 세 번째 별에서는 술고래를 만났다. 부끄러운 것을 잊으려고 술을 마시고 또 술을 마시는 것이 부끄러워 술을 마신다는 무기력한 술꾼을 어린 왕자는 이해할 수 없어 한다. 네 번째 별에서 만난 실업가는 숫자만 세고 있었다.

하늘의 별마저 소유하고 싶어 안달인 그는 소유의 욕망에 사로잡힌 어른의 상징이다. 가장 작은 별인 다섯 번째 별에서 가로등을 켜는 사람은 맹목적이고 부조리한 어른의 표상으로 비쳤다. 여섯 번째 별에서 만난 지리학자는 허황된 지식분자로 보였다. 이런 별들을 거쳐 지리학자의 권유로 어린 왕자는 일곱 번째 별로 지구를 택한다.

지구는 "111명의 왕(분명히 흑인 왕까지 넣어서)과 7천 명의 지리학자, 90만 명의 실업가, 750만 명의 술고래, 3억 천백단 명의 젠 체하는 사람들, 즉 모두 합해서 약 20억의 어른들이 살고" 있는 커다란 별이었다. 이런 어른의 생태는 인간다움의 본성에서 멀어진 세계다. 어린 왕자가 보기에는 참으로 이상한 세계다. 일상적으로 늘 되풀이되는 현상을 놓고 이상한 세계라고 얘기함으로써 본질적 반성을 촉구하는 셈이다.

▶ 보이지 않는 심연에서의 책임과 배려

어린 왕자는 자신의 소혹성에서 장미를 길들이다 속상해서 떠나왔다. 장미는 때때로 아무렇게나 말하고 요구했다. 때로 거짓말을 하다가 부끄러워서 얼버무리기도 했다. 어린 왕자는 자기가 길들인 장미지만, 장미의 이런저런 태도 때문에 장미에게 공감하거나 동정하지 않았다. 그래서 장미를 떠나왔던 것이다. 그런데 어린 왕자는 그것을 후회한다.

> 사실 나는 아무것도 이해할 줄 몰랐어. 꽃이 하는 말이 아니라 행동으로 판단했어야 했는데. 꽃은 나에게 향기를 뿜어 주었고 눈부신 아름다움을 보여 주었는데. …그 불쌍한 말 뒤엔 따뜻한 마음이 숨어 있는 걸 눈치 챘어야 했는데.

그러면서 "하긴 난 꽃을 사랑하기엔 너무 어렸어"라고 말하기도 한다. 장미가 겉으로 드러낸 말이 아니라 보이지 않는 장미의 심연을 보았어야 했다는 어린 왕자의 반성적 사유는 매우 도저하다. 그렇지 않은가. 세상의 많은 인간관계는 바로 이런 지점에서 그릇되지 않던가. 세상의 많은 다툼과 시기, 미움과 결별이 이런 심연의 눈 혹은 심연의 사유 내지 심연의 배려의 결여에서 비롯되지 않았던가 말이다. 이렇게 반성적 사유를 길어 올릴 줄 아는 어린 왕자에게 여우는 책임의 윤리를 거듭 강조한다. "당신은 당신이 길들인 것에 대해서는 끝까지 책임을 져야 하는 거예요. 당신의 장미에게 당신은 책임이 있어요."

책임과 배려를 위해서는 보이지 않는 심연을 성찰할 수 있는 심안을 지녀야 한다. 화자는 이 점을 거듭 강조한다. "집이건 별이건, 사막이건 그들을 아름답게 하는 것은 눈에 보이지 않는 거야!" 그렇다. 어린 왕자도 그랬었다. "중요한 것은 눈에 보이지 않는 거야." 그러면 어떻게 할 것인가. 우리는 심연의 심안을 회복해야 한다. 우리가 본래 지니고 있던 것이되, 일상적이고 세속적인 삶에서 잃어버린 것, 바로 어린 왕자는 눈을 회복해야 하는 것이다. 그 눈의 회복을 위해 우리는 부단히 탐구해야 함을 작가는 아울러 강조한다.

"어린 왕자는 한 번 묻기 시작하면 답을 얻을 때까지 묻지 않고는 못 견디는 성미였다." 같은 부분에서 명료하듯, 묻고 또 물어야 한다. 정녕 인간적인 것의 상실과 회복과 관한 우주적 드라마를 《어린 왕자》는 연출해 보인다. 그런 면에서 이 작품은 오래된 미래의 진실과 통하는 신화다. 그 신화를 통해 인간은 본원적인 삶을 새롭게 꿈꿀 수 있는 가능성을 열게 된다. 꿈은 진실한 존재 정립의 가능성과 아울러 고정 관념과 인습의 틀을 넘어선 역동적 창조성의 밑거름이 된다. 《어린 왕자》를 통해 우주적 동경과 인간적 진실의 신화를 넉넉하게 가늠해 보고 새롭게 꿈꿀 수 있는 사람은 행복할 것이다.